Christopher G. Tiedeman

The unwritten Constitution of the United States

A philosophical Inquiry into the Fundamentals of American constitutional Law

Christopher G. Tiedeman

The unwritten Constitution of the United States
A philosophical Inquiry into the Fundamentals of American constitutional Law

ISBN/EAN: 9783337062255

Printed in Europe, USA, Canada, Australia, Japan

Cover: Foto ©ninafisch / pixelio.de

More available books at **www.hansebooks.com**

THE UNWRITTEN CONSTITUTION OF THE UNITED STATES

A PHILOSOPHICAL INQUIRY INTO THE FUNDAMENTALS OF AMERICAN CONSTITUTIONAL LAW

BY

CHRISTOPHER G. TIEDEMAN, A.M., LL.B.

PROFESSOR OF LAW IN THE UNIVERSITY OF MISSOURI
AUTHOR OF TREATISES ON "THE LIMITATIONS OF POLICE POWER," "THE LAW OF REAL PROPERTY," AND "LAW OF COMMERCIAL PAPER"

G. P. PUTNAM'S SONS

NEW YORK   LONDON
27 WEST TWENTY-THIRD ST.   27 KING WILLIAM ST., STRAND
The Knickerbocker Press
1890

The Knickerbocker Press, New York
Electrotyped, Printed, and Bound by
G. P. Putnam's Sons

CONTENTS

THE UNWRITTEN CONSTITUTION
OF THE UNITED STATES.

CHAPTER I.

ORIGIN AND DEVELOPMENT OF MUNICIPAL LAW IN GENERAL.

BLACKSTONE'S definition of law has been generally accepted as in the main reliable, not only
popularly, but also professionally. Indeed, the scientific element of the definition, viz. : that municipal
law is "a rule of conduct *prescribed by the supreme
power of the state*," has been so earnestly accentuated
and elaborated by the master-minds who have truly
dominated legal thought in England and in this
country for the past half century—I refer, of course,
to Bentham and Austin,—that the professional, as
well as the popular, mind has been led into the
adoption, as an axiomatic truth, of a most serious
error concerning the origin and development of municipal law.

Except in the matter of form, the statement that municipal law is " prescribed by the supreme power of the state " is false and misleading, unless by the " supreme power of the state " is meant the aggregation of all the social forces, both material and spiritual, which go to make up our civilization. But the meaning commonly attached to the words " the supreme power of the state " is that of the supreme power in the government, as distinguished from the people who compose the body politic. Austin and his followers admit that the law-making power is subject to moral and physical restraints, and that these restraints co-operate very largely in forming and modifying the substantive law ; but since no rule can be called a law, which is not enforced by a sanction, prescribed by the law-making power, the moral influences at work upon society cannot be said to create law. And even where a rule of law is for the first time enunciated by an English or American court, Austin claims that it first became a law when the court announced its decision. I do not suppose Austin intended to assert that the decision of the court was purely arbitrary ; that it only reflected the sentiments of the occupants of the judicial bench. I cannot believe that he was unconscious of the natural sequential development of the law, operated upon by all the social forces, out of which civilization is in general evolved. But the reader of his work on jurisprudence will have no very clear conception of this scientific development if he has not obtained the idea elsewhere. The rigid logic of Austin is inclined to fasten upon the reader the more or less popular superstition concerning the omnipotence of the law-making power.

Undoubtedly there is no living law without a sanction or penalty, and there must be somewhere some one who has the power to inflict the penalty. The law is intended to force upon a rebellious minority the observance of those rules of conduct the infractions of which will inflict injury upon others. Physical force is of course needed. Hence the blindfolded Goddess of Justice not only holds up in her left hand the scales with which she can impartially mete out justice between parties litigant, but she also bears in her strong right hand the sword, which she must wield with effect, in order to enforce her decrees. If a decree of the court is to be enforced, the sheriff, who is the local representative of the executive department of the government, summons his *posse comitatus, i.e.,* he calls upon the good and law-abiding citizens of the county to support him, and none can lawfully refuse to obey the call.

But granting that to make a rule of conduct a law a penalty must be attached and imposed for its infraction, it does not necessarily follow that that penalty must be enforced by an organized government, or that its enforcement by such a government essentially changes the character of the rule. When the English colonists first made their settlement in this country, we are told they brought with them the English common-law, and enforced it among themselves, so far as that law was compatible with the surrounding circumstances. If one of the colonists had made an attack upon the person or property of another, before there had been any organized government, armed with the power to enforce the law, would the Austin school of jurists claim that these colonists were without law, and hence this reprehensible deed was not illegal? Would they claim that there was no law on the borders of American civilization, where the only government is the vigilance committee, and where the only court of justice is presided over by Judge Lynch? If a man is murdered or a horse stolen in such a community, and the offender is captured by the vigilance committee, tried by Judge Lynch, and punished in accordance with the custom of the country, he has suffered the penalty of the law, as much as the criminal in an orderly, more civilized community, who is tried and condemned by a regularly organized court, and punished by the ordinary administrative officers of the government. The only difference between the two cases is the degree of development in the administration of the law. Lynch-law, in a community not possessed of a properly organized government, is as much law as the enactment of an American legislature or the acts of Parliament. Nor is there any greater difference in the character of the forces which in their operations upon the social life command the formulation and enforcement of the rules of conduct in the two cases. In both cases the average common-sense of propriety, which is uniformly obeyed by the vast majority of a people, constitutes in the main the standard after which rules of law are modelled. The morality commonly and uniformly practised by the masses lends its character to the rule of law when it is first enunciated. And even when the rule is first promulgated, its ethical character is much lower than the standard of morality set up by ethical teachers ; for only that code of morality can be enforced against delinquents which the people generally obey. For if it were attempted to enforce a higher standard, for example, to compel every one to *do unto others as he would have them do unto him*, the sanction would be wanting, for no penalty is effective unless it is backed by the *posse comitatus.*

Municipal law is not intended to control the actions of the masses. The great majority of a people are a law unto themselves. And wherever this fundamental thought is lost sight of, legislation results in nothing but the production of dead letters, still-born laws, that never did and never could have become a living rule of conduct. For the life of a rule of law is derived from its habitual and spontaneous observance by the mass of the people. It is only when its enactment is called for by a popular sense of necessity, in order to compel a rebellious minority to conform to the moral habits and customs of the people, that a rule of conduct can become a living law. Although a moment's reflection is sufficient to satisfy one of the correctness of this position, it is surprising what false notions of legislation do prevail, even among scientific men. The tenets of a large and influential school of economists are based, confessedly or otherwise, upon the notion that the living power of the law is from an extra-human source; for they are preaching the doctrine daily that the ills of life, which they admit to be the consequences of sin and ignorance, or, in other words, of the frailties of human nature, may be cured or, at least, lessened by legislation, even where the evil is not the result of a trespass. And the call is often made for fresh legislation, as a means of raising the standard of morality of the people. The stream can never rise higher than its source, nor can it be expected that legal rules, which are but a reflection of the moral habits of a people, can effect their moral elevation; least of all, the moral elevation of a people living under a government "of the people, for the people, and by the people." One may just as well expect by taking thought to add one cubit unto his stature, as by legislative declaration to add one cubit to the moral stature of the people.

The legal rule is, therefore, fashioned after the prevalent sense of right. The Germans call it *Rechtsgefuehl.*

It is not so difficult for the novice to admit this doctrine in its application to judicial legislation, or judge-made law, as Bentham contemptuously calls it; but it is more difficult to believe that the legislative will is bound down by this prevalent sense of right to a fixed line of conduct, from which it cannot successfully swerve. I do not mean to say that the legislature cannot make an enactment, which does not reflect the prevalent sense of right; for there are too many deplorable instances of such misuse of power, to admit of denial.[1] But I do assert emphatically that the legislature cannot completely enslave the popular will by an enactment not endorsed by the prevalent sense of right. Popular opinion, for prudential reasons, requires of the individual obedience to the written word, until the power which enacted

---

[1] The expression "deplorable misuse of power" is used in this connection, because the writer is convinced that the multiplication of laws which cannot be enforced tends to lessen the popular reverence or respect for law, and habituates the people to the repeated violation, not only of those laws which do not reflect the prevalent sense of right, but also those which are so sanctioned.

it can be induced or forced to repeal it. To this extent can the legislative will, as a factor in the making of the law, influence its development in opposition to the popular desire. But when the law is brought before the courts for enforcement, its practical operation will be made by interpretation and construction to conform to the prevalent sense of right, as far as this is possible without nullifying the letter of the law. It frequently happens that the effect of the statute will in this manner be completely changed, and will, as it is enforced, produce an entirely different effect from what had been intended. A most notable example is the English Statute of Uses. This statute was enacted for the purpose of abolishing uses entirely, and preventing the creation of any equitable interest in lands, separate and apart from the legal title. But when this statute was brought before the courts, it met with the most determined opposition from the bench and bar. They reflected the prevalent sense of right in the middle English classes, and gave the statute a strict technical construction, thus limiting its operation to such an extent that, instead of being abolished by the statute, the law of uses became all the more firmly settled. Upon this distorting, technical construction of the English Statute of Uses rests the entire law of modern trusts, except so far as there have been modifications by American statutes. Instances of this kind may be multipled indefinitely.

It may, therefore, be laid down as a general proposition that a legal rule is the product of social forces, reflecting the prevalent sense of right.   It is another question, what is the relative influence of individuals and of classes in moulding this popular sense of right. The state of the public mind may be such that it may be said of that people, *quod principi placuit habet legis vigorem;* and even in the land of democratic rule and of universal suffrage, only a few persons really mould and fashion public opinion.   The great body of private law is, by common consent, usually left to be developed by the legal profession.   Still, in every country, it matters not how or by whom it is created, whatever is the prevalent sense of right is the norm by which legal rules are formulated.

But the popular sense of right does not remain stationary.   In its growth and evolution it follows an easily recognized law of development.   The popular sense of right rises with the increasing enlightenment of the ethical teachers.   Although the legal rule reflects the popular sense of right, prevalent when it was formulated, it may not, and usually does not, conform altogether to the popular sense of right in its later stages of development, and very frequently there is so great a variance between them as to cause serious popular dissatisfaction.

Philosophical enthusiasts sometimes claim that this variance is due to the imperfect formulation of the legal rule, and that but for this imperfect reflection of the prevalent sense of right by the formulated rule legal rules would never conflict with public sentiment in any stage of its development. Be this as it may, there is such a variance which increases with the ethical and spiritual development of the people.

A very good example of this variance between the existing rule of law and the popular sense of right is to be found in the law of fraud. The existing rules of law declare that a transaction is not tainted by fraud if one of the parties is induced to enter into it by a mistaken appreciation of the material facts, simply because the other party knew of the first party's misapprehension and failed to give him the desired information. For example, if A. is offering to buy an article of value from B., and believing that the article is worth one thousand dollars, being led to that conclusion by the belief that the article has merits which it does not possess, when in fact it is not worth more than five hundred dollars ; if B. has said or done nothing to produce that wrong impression, he can take the excessive price, without being guilty of legal fraud, although he knows at the time that the value of the subject-matter of the sale has been greatly over-estimated by A. When that rule was first formulated, I have no doubt that tradesmen and others habitually practised the rule of taking advantage of the ignorance of others, whenever they had done nothing to create the ignorance or to prevent the acquisition of the necessary knowledge; and it is, without doubt, still the general rule of conduct in the more subtle business transactions of the day. But in the balder and more transparent cases of the kind described, the influence of the teaching of a higher morality is being felt so as to prevent a very large number, if not a majority, of the people from practising upon their weaker brethren what is certainly a moral, if not a legal, fraud. This deviation of a large part of the people from the directions of the existing rule of law is, however, not yet strong enough to require any material modification of it; but it is sufficiently strong to involve in doubt the correctness of the enunciated rule. The people do not yet spontaneously and habitually follow the higher rule. Whenever this radical change in the habits of the people does come about, then, and not till then, may we expect the legal rule to conform to the better teaching of morality.

So far nothing has been said to accentuate the fact that this change in the prevalent sense of right is not the quiet, smooth, uneventful development, which is found to prevail in the growth of a language, and which is claimed by the jurists of the Savigny-Puchta school to prevail in the growth of a system of jurisprudence.

On the contrary, the history of the law demonstrates conclusively, by a host of examples, that every material modification of an existing principle of law, as well as every new principle of law, is never firmly fixed in the jurisprudence of a country except after a vigorous contest between opposing forces.[1]

As soon as a legal rule has been formulated, private interests begin to be built up in reliance upon the application of this formulated rule to all future similar cases. Unless there were some fixity and certainty in the rules of law, there could be no material development, no inducement to individual activity. These private interests, thus developed, are concerned in the strict enforcement of the formulated rule, and resist all changes in word or in spirit. In obedience to this popular desire for fixity and certainty, the letter of the law, as formulated by the courts, receives by popular agreement the same binding authority, as is freely conceded to the statute. The rule of *stare decisis* prevents subsequent courts from completely repealing the rule of law previously formulated, even though, on account of a change in popular sentiment, the law should cease to reflect the prevalent sense of right. If by means of fictional construction

---

[1] " Das Ziel des Rechts ist der Friede, das Mittel dazu der Kampf. . . . Das Leben des Rechts ist Kampf, ein Kampf der Völker— der Staatgewalt—der Stände—der Individuen. Alles Recht in der Welt ist erstritten worden, jeder Rechtssatz, der da gilt, hat erst denen, die sich ihm widersetzten, abgerungen werden müssen, und jedes Recht, das Recht eines Volkes, wie das eines Einzelnen, setzt die stetige Bereitschaft zu seiner Behauptung voraus."—v. Ihering's Kampf um's Recht, 1.

the letter of the law cannot be made to conform to the existing sense of right, and the variance is so great as to cause great discomfort or arouse the disapprobation of the people, the only remedy is a change by legislative enactment. But this rule of *stare decisis* is absolutely binding, only as it also reflects the prevalent sense of right. Cases have frequently occurred when the variance between the law and the prevalent sense of right was so distressing that the courts have been justified by public sentiment in abrogating an established rule. In such cases the judges have sought refuge under the fiction that the prior decision was an erroneous statement of the pre-existing law; and hence in every law library are to be found collections of "overruled cases." But it not unfrequently happens that even this elastic fiction will not furnish any actual justification for the abrogation of the existing rule of law; and yet it is done in compliance with the demand of private interest or the popular sense of justice. Still the case must be an urgent one, in order to meet with popular approval. As a general rule, public sentiment requires a rigid adherence to the rule "*stare decisis.*"

It must be further observed, that not every moral rule commonly practised by the mass of people, becomes a legal rule, obedience to which is enforced by a legal sanction. Unless the violation of the

moral rule involves some injury to the public or
to other persons, there is never any public demand
for its enforcement by the imposition of a legal penalty. Those wrongful, immoral acts, which are properly called crimes or trespasses upon the interests of
others, are generally regulated by law, but, except so
far as they likewise have the character of trespasses,
vices are left to the correction of the moral influence
of public opinion. The world is moved and controlled
by two fundamentally different forces, moral suasion
and physical force. While different, they need not be
antagonistic, and only are so when the physical force
is employed to attain some unrighteous end. These
forces are supplementary to each other, and one cannot take the place of the other. The effect of moral
suasion is to build up or reform the character of the
person or persons intended to be influenced. Physical force can only be used successfully to suppress
the desire and intention to do injury to others. You
cannot expect to make a virtuous man out of a criminal by sending him to the penitentiary or to the
whipping-post. The only end attained by such
measures is the prevention of future crime by creating the fear of punishment. Vice therefore cannot
be successfully controlled by any measures of force;
the correction must be left to the moral suasion of
the church, the home, and the social circle. But
when the peace and good order of society are threat-

ened by attacks upon the personal security, personal liberty, and property of others there is nothing to do but to repel force by force. Of course this repressive force can, in an orderly community, be employed only by the government, except in the few cases of emergency where the right of self-defence is conceded to the individual.

I believe I have succeeded in showing that the same social forces which create and develop the ethics of a nation create and develop its law ; that the substantive law is essentially nothing more than the moral rules, commonly and habitually obeyed by the masses, whose enforcement by the courts is required for the public good, while ethics are the rules of morality set forth by our moral teachers, as their highest conceptions of moral development. The morality of the law is commonly and habitually practised by the people ; the morality of ethics, if this expression be allowed me, is an idealistic conception, something to be striven for, and more and more approximated, but perhaps never to be fully realized before the days of the millennium.

CHAPTER II.

THE ORIGIN AND DEVELOPMENT OF CONSTITUTIONAL LAW.

THE constitution of a state may be described as the definition of the order and structure of the body politic, while constitutional law consists of those fundamental principles and rules in accordance with which the government is constructed and its orderly administration is conducted. Constitutional law may be described as the anatomy and physiology of the body politic.

If these definitions be accepted as true, the conclusion is irresistible that the fundamental principles which form the constitution of a state cannot be created by any governmental or popular edict; they are necessarily found imbedded in the national character and are developed in accordance with the national growth. This doctrine is admitted in its application to the so-called unwritten constitutions, like that of England, whose changes are effected by ordinary parliamentary action, and which cannot be found in any one written instrument, but whose prin-

ciples are to be found scattered along the pathway of
the nation's history, and serving more or less as land-
marks to indicate its political growth.   The English
Constitution is to be found in the *Magna Charta*, the
Petition of Right, the *Habeas Corpus* act, and the
Bill of Rights.   It is plain to the most superficial
observer that the English Constitution was not the
conscious and voluntary creation of the English people ; that it was an evolution from the simple political principles and formulæ of the Teutonic race,
finding its beginning in the tribal government of the
German barbarians, so graphically described by Taci-
tus.   But when the so-called written constitutions of
America and Europe, which are promulgated by the
supreme power of the respective countries in the
form of a single instrument, and which become
operative from the time of their publication, come
under consideration, the impulse of all, and the conviction of the many, ascribe to them a very different
origin.   Even one of the most distinguished statesmen, if not the most distinguished statesman, of
modern times, Mr. Gladstone, falls into the grave
error of claiming for these two kinds of constitutions
a different origin and a different rule of development, when he says that "just as the British Constitution is the most subtle organism which has proceeded from progressive history, so the American
Constitution is the most wonderful work ever struck

2

off at a given time by the brain and purpose of man." It is very true that the attempts to create constitutions off-hand, and to establish them over a people to whom the fundamental principles of the proposed constitutions are an unknown tongue, have been frequent; but it will be impossible to point out a single instance where such a constitution became a permanent and living rule of conduct. Constitutions are effective only so far as their principles have their roots imbedded in the national character, and consequently constitute a faithful reflection of the national will. The Japanese nation has lately adopted a written constitution, after a study of the various constitutional governments of Europe and America; very many principles of the constitutions of the German and English empires, as well as of the American Constitution, have been incorporated into it. But notwithstanding the wonderful adaptiveness of the Japanese character to political and economic innovations, it remains to be seen how much of their new constitution will prove effective, and how much will become inoperative. So far as the principles of their constitution are an outcome of the existing Japanese civilization, and consequently strike a responsive chord in the national heart, will the constitution prove a permanent and living rule of conduct. It is, of course, to be remembered that the Japanese reverence for the authority of the Mikado, and the long-established national habit of unquestioning obedience to the imperial commands, will go far towards stifling popular discontent, or dissipating any want of harmony with the principles and rules of the new constitution, which many will consider and receive as the commands of the august Mikado. But as soon as the people become conscious of their own power, and their reverence for imperial decrees becomes lessened by a more intimate acquaintance with the principles of self-government and democratic rule, the untrammelled political sentiment of the nation will mould the existing constitution into harmonious correspondence, or demand its complete abolition or revision.

History furnishes numerous examples of fruitless attempts to impose constitutions upon people whose principles are not in harmony with the popular political sentiment. Locke prepared a written constitution for the Carolinas, whose principles were not in harmony with the popular instinct; Napoleon Bonaparte prepared paper constitutions for the nations whom he conquered, and unhappy France, refusing to believe that " constitutions are not made, they grow," has had one constitution after another, in her effort to secure an orderly and permanent establishment for a republican government. And it is not difficult to comprehend that the failure or success of a form of constitution and government in the experience of one people does not indicate any inherent and universal demerits or excellences, or assure a similar experience if they are adopted by some other people. Englishmen and Americans are so infatuated with the superior qualities of their constitutions that in their canonization of them they are led to believe that their principles are of universal application, and are surprised if a foreigner criticises them from the standpoint of foreign needs and experience. The English and American constitutions work well, and challenge the admiration of political students, not because of their inherent and abstract excellences—for it would be no arduous or insuperable task to point out several glaring defects,[1] but because they are in complete correspondence with the political sentiment of the respective nations, and are themselves the natural products of Anglo-American civilization. It is not so much what is found in the written constitution, as the conservative, law-abiding, and yet liberty-loving character of the Anglo-Saxon, which guarantees a permanent free government to England and to the United States of America.

What gives color to the notion that the American constitutions, both State and Federal, are the voluntary creation of man, is the fact that they are written (so-called), and that these writings have been formulated, enacted, and promulgated by representative conventions. This opinion has been so prevalent,

---

[1] See many passages in Bryce's "American Commonwealths."

that the national habit is to look upon the members
of the convention of 1787 as demigods, giant heroes,
far surpassing the foremost men of to-day, while the
Constitution itself has been placed upon a pedestal
and worshipped as a popular idol. It is very far from
my purpose to deny to the heroes of the Revolution
their just meed of praise, or to subject the Federal
Constitution to any hostile or carping criticism. It
is, without doubt, the best political constitution that
the world has ever seen, and some of its fundamental principles are worthy of universal adoption. But
by making a popular idol of it, we are apt to lose
the very benefits which its excellences insure. It
is the complete harmony of its principles with the
political evolution of the nation, which justly challenges our admiration, and not the political acumen
of the convention which promulgated it. Instead,
therefore, of being the voluntary creation of the
American people of the eighteenth century, the Federal and State constitutions of the United States are
but natural sequential developments of the British
Constitution, modified as to detail and as to a few
fundamental principles by the new environment.
This claim is easily substantiated by the most superficial comparison of the British and American constitutions.

Without making minute reference to the close
similarity of the town and county organizations under these constitutions, the lineal descent of the

American constitutional law from the British finds proof in the fact that in both nations the attachment to the principles of local government challenges the attention and admiration of the critic.   Under both systems of constitutional law we find an unvarying determination to confine the exercise of governmental power to the local authorities in every thing affecting only the local interests; and if there is any material difference in respect to the scope of local powers, it is to be found to consist of a greater localization of power under the British Constitution, in this, that the taxation for local purposes is in Great Britain invariably within the control of the county, while in the United States the taxes for the same purposes, outside of corporate towns and cities, although expended in the county in which they are collected, are imposed by the legislature, unless the power of taxation is expressly conferred upon the local authorities.[1]

---

[1] "From time immemorial the counties, parishes, towns, and territorial subdivisions of the country have been allowed in England, and, indeed, required to lay rates on themselves for local purposes. . . . From the foundation of our government, colonial and republican, the necessary sums for local purposes have been raised by the people or authorities at home.   Court-houses, prisons, bridges, poorhouses, and the like, are thus built and kept up, and the expenses of maintaining the poor, and of prosecutions and jurors, are thus defrayed, and of late (in North Carolina) a portion of the common school fund and a provision for the indigent insane are thus raised, while the highways are altogether constructed and repaired by local labor, distributed under the orders of the county magistrates."—Ruffin, J., in Caldwell *v.* Justices, etc., 4 Jones (N. C.), Eq., 323.

While the spirit of local government is so far obeyed, in the matter of taxation for local purposes, that one county or other corporate district cannot be taxed for the local purposes of another county or district, and the money collected on a local tax must be expended in the same county or district, yet in the absence of express legislative authority, the American constitutional law denies to such local authorities the power to impose the tax.[1] But with this exception—which is accountable only on the theory advanced by Mr. Taylor,[2] that this doctrine of local government was lost sight of in the general prevalence and application of the political notion that all legislative power was limited to an express grant of powers, except the power of the State General Assembly—it is manifest that local government in the United States is a reproduction of the local government of Great Britain. And there has been so little change in the character and powers of the local government officers, that one can obtain a very

---

[1] Cooley's Const. Lim. (230), 283 (488), 605 ; Litchfield *v.* Vernon, 41 N. Y., 132 ; Mobile & S. H. R. Co., *v.* Kennerly, 74 Ala., 574; Booth *v.* Woodbury, 32 Conn., 118 ; Speer *v.* School Dist., 50 Pa. St., 150. And the levy for local purposes may be ordered by the legislature, not only without the consent, but against the wishes, of the people concerned. Cheaney *v.* Hooser, 9 B. Mon., 330 ; Slack *v.* Maysville, etc., R. R. Co., 1-3 B. Mon., 1 ; Cypress Pond Draining Co. *v.* Hooper, 2 Met. (Ky.), 350.

[2] "Origin and Growth of the English Constitution," by Hannis Taylor, p. 43.

reliable account of the powers and duties of the American sheriff, coroner, constable, justice of the peace, etc., by reading Mr. Blackstone's chapter on inferior administrative officers.

The fundamental division of governmental powers into executive, legislative, and judicial, and their exercise by separate and independent departments of the government, form a striking characteristic of both the English and American constitutions. Even before they had emerged from the colonial state, the Americans had adopted this doctrine, and divided their local governments into executive, legislative, and judicial departments, conceding to each department the powers exercised by the corresponding department of the English government. The executive, for many reasons other than the existence of an anti-monarchical spirit, could only obtain the essential powers of the English executive, without its form and tenure of office. But the legislature was fashioned in close imitation of Parliament, with its two co-ordinate chambers, with the single variation that in the upper house the elective principle was substituted for the hereditary principle ; while the judiciary not only exercised the same powers as the English judiciary, but administered justice under the same forms of procedure, and in courts established on the English itinerant system, viz.: the holding of court in each county by a judge, to whom was assigned a particular circuit, composed of one or more counties.

When the present Federal Constitution was adopted, the same salient features were given to the Federal Government, so that one is justified in saying, that a detailed review of the powers of the various departments of the government both Federal and State, forces one to the conclusion that the American constitutions are, in the main, an evolutionary development of the British Constitution[1]; and a closer study of the two systems reveals the fact that every principle, brought into play by the American constitutions, that has endured, and proved effectual in the attainment of the ends aimed at, was either of English origin, or was the direct product of the social forces then at play in American life.

Nor is it surprising that the American constitutions should be fashioned in imitation of the British Constitution. Not only were the men who led and formed public opinion in the colonies thoroughly acquainted with English constitutional law, many of them having been born or educated in the United

---

[1] " When all of these elements of likeness are considered, who can fail to perceive that the typical English state in America is, in a constitutional sense, simply the English kingdom transferred to a new theatre, where it has entered upon a wider destiny, with its political horizon unclouded by the waning shadows of nobility, feudality, and kingship."—Taylor's " Origin and Growth of the English Constitution," p. 48.

Kingdom,[1] but the universal political sentiment, under the influence of Montesquieu, also pronounced the British Constitution, if not absolutely perfect, at least the best the world ever knew.[2] Blackstone's Commentaries and Montesquieu's " Esprit des Lois " were the two books which the students of political science of that day consulted in the handling of social problems. The American constitutions could not,

---

[1] " The Virginia delegation (to the constitutional convention of 1787) was simply a brilliant group of English country gentlemen who had been reared on the right side of the Atlantic.   Alexander Hamilton and Robert Morris were born English subjects ; the father of Franklin was an English emigrant from Northamptonshire ; Charles Cotesworth Pinckney had been educated at Oxford and the Middle Temple ; Rutledge had studied law at the Temple ; and James Wilson, the most far-sighted man perhaps in the whole convention, was born near St. Andrews, in Scotland.   As to political training, they had all been reared under the English system of local self-government which had grown up alongside of the English customary law in the several States which they represented.   These States they had helped to transform from English provinces into independent commonwealths whose constitutions were substantial reproductions of that of the English kingdom.   In fine, the only practical conception of the State which they possessed was that embodied in the constitution of the old land, modified as it had been in the new by the abolition of nobility, feudality, and kingship."—Taylor's " Origin and Growth of the English Constitution," p. 62.

[2] " The British Constitution was to Montesquieu what Homer had been to the didactic writers on epic poetry.   As the latter have considered the work of the immortal bard as the perfect model from which the principles and rules of the epic art were to be drawn, and by which all similar works were to be judged ; so this great political critic appears to have viewed the Constitution of England as the standard, or, to use his own expression, as the mirror, of political liberty."—*Federalist*, No. xlvii, p. 300.

therefore, be any thing else but adaptations of the British Constitution.

In the formation of the Federal Constitution other forces were at work, which compelled some slight and some radical departures from the English forms. In the struggles of the colonies against the unjust encroachments of the mother-country on their right of self-government, they had united in congresses called for the consideration of their common welfare; but until the actual outbreak of hostilities, the Congress had not attempted the assertion or exercise of any superior or superintending control of the colonies. All the actions of the congresses were recommendatory in form and fact. But with the publication of the Declaration of Independence, Congress did assume many of the powers of a superior government, especially the general conduct of the war with England and of intercourse with the foreign powers. The government, thus established, was of course revolutionary, and remained so until the Articles of Confederation were adopted by the States and put into operation. The fact that there had been no legal union of the colonies, except through their common subjection to England, coupled with the dread and hatred of all external or superior governments, which had been engendered by England's tyrannical exercise of her power, had accustomed the popular mind to the thought that each State was supreme, and that their liberty depended upon the retention of this state supremacy, combining with each other in the capacity of sovereign states, only as far as this was necessary for the common defence or promotive of the general welfare.

The educated men of that day were classical scholars, and were acquainted with the previous attempts made to establish federal government; but, according to the knowledge then had of these attempts, all of them had resulted in the establishment of nothing more than a league, while the several members of the league retained their supreme powers. Under these circumstances it was but natural that their ignorance of the great possibilities of federal government should combine, with their dread of foreign or external governments, to create a league, instead of a centralized state. Hence the Articles of Confederation contained very meagre grants of powers to the general government; and in no instance was the general government permitted to exercise any control over the individual citizen, every decree of Congress being a requisition upon the States, which Congress had not the power to enforce, and which the States complied with or ignored, as they pleased.

A government, so weak that it did not even command the respect of the people, much less their obedience, could not last long. Every thoughtful man of the day was impressed with the gravity of the situation, and looked forward to the future with the most anxious forebodings. Internal dissensions and local prejudices, intense love of local government, and an implacable hatred of any superior power, co-operated to make anarchy apparently inevitable, and justify the claim "that the most critical period of the country's history embraced the time between 1783 and the adoption of the Constitution in 1788."[1] The forces of disintegration were so strong that any more perfect union was despaired of. It was only by a gradual and diplomatic approach to the end in view that the adoption of the present Constitution was secured. The first step taken was the cession to the general government of the lands in the limitless and unexplored West, to be held and administered as a common fund for the benefit of all the States. From the necessity of the case, the general government thus acquired a dignity and respectability of character which it did not possess before, and the necessary assumption of supreme power over this vast territory, however small the practical exercise of authority was, accustomed the people somewhat to

---

[1] Trescot's "Diplomatic History of the Administrations of Washington and Adams," p. 9. See also, to the same effect, John Fiske's "Critical Period of American History, 1783-1789," which gives a brilliant exposition of American struggle for national unity.

the possession by the general government of the powers of sovereignty; while the existence of this large territory as a common fund served in itself, through the promptings of self-interest, to strengthen the tie that bound the States together. The credit of this initial step towards the establishment of a permanent union of the States is due to Maryland, who persistently refused to sign the Articles of Confederation until she was assured of the cession of these lands to the Union.

The next step was the formation by Virginia and Maryland, under the inspiration of Washington, of a joint commission for the mutual control of the navigation of the Potomac River. Inasmuch as the control of this river would involve more or less the control of the Ohio, whose head-waters joined with those of the Potomac, Pennsylvania was invited to join with the other two States in this commission. Other matters of common concern, such as the regulation of the currency and other commercial regulations, were suggested for consideration by this commission. After some delay, and as a result of these efforts of union for commercial and economical purposes, the Virginia legislature passed a motion, inviting all the States to appoint commissioners to meet at Annapolis for the consideration of the best method of securing a uniform regulation of commerce. The attendance at the Annapolis convention was not large enough to enable any effective action to be taken, and, after much discussion, the commissioners adopted a resolution urging the appointment of commissioners, to convene in Philadelphia in the following May, " to devise such further provisions as shall appear to them necessary to render the Constitution of the federal government adequate to the exigencies of the Union, and to report to Congress such an act as, when agreed to by them, and confirmed by the legislatures of every State, would effectually provide the same."

Congress did not immediately agree to this proposition for a convention, but the suffering of the people, and their growing discontent, followed by frequent riotous outbreaks of the most serious sort, finally compelled Congress to take the necessary action, and a resolution was adopted, recommending a convention in Philadelphia, in May, 1787, of delegates from the States " for the purpose of revising the Articles of Confederation, and reporting to Congress and the several legislatures such alterations and provisions therein as shall, when agreed to in Congress and confirmed by the States, under the Federal Constitution, be adequate to the exigencies of government and the preservation of the Union." [1]

---

[1] See Chapter V. of Mr. Fiske's " Critical Period of American History," entitled " Germs of National Sovereignty," for a very interesting and graphic account of the growth of the demand for a more effective national government.

But the local pride and prejudices of the people were not the only serious obstacles in the way of an increase of the powers of the Federal Government, which fell short of a complete extinction of the States as independent bodies politic. It was idle to advocate the absorption of the States into one composite state. The people would have rejected such a proposition with vehemence and indignation. And yet history had never produced a federal government which was not a league. The Federal Union, under the Articles of Confederation, was only a league, and neither claimed nor exercised any authority over the individual citizen. The experience of the people under these Articles of Confederation had demonstrated the futility of the attempt of the Federal Government to assume the powers of government, without the ability and right to compel the obedience of the individual to its commands ; and yet the past experience of the world suggested no relief or remedy. It was reserved for an American to create an absolutely new political idea of the most transcendent importance, and which has ultimately solved the problem of combining a strong central government with an independent local government.

In February, 1783, Pelatial Webster published "A Dissertation on the Political Union and Constitution of the Thirteen United States of North America,"

which was a year later followed by another of the
same tenor, by Noah Webster, in both of which was
proposed " a new system of government which should
act, *not on the States, but directly on individuals,* and
vest in Congress full power to carry its laws into
effect." When we consider for a moment the won-
derfulness of two separate and in many respects independent governmental agencies exerting their powers over the same territory, and each within its own
sphere commanding the obedience of the same people, there is no occasion for surprise that it required
a century of experience under the new government
to fully appreciate its significance and effect. The
successful maintenance of the separate autonomy of
the Federal and State governments for a century,
through all the vicissitudes of political fortune which
fell to the lot of the people of the United States,
furnished an enigmatical contradiction of the prevalent notions of an indivisible sovereignty.[1]

If there be such a thing in politics as sovereignty,
it is necessarily indivisible, and hence it is impossible
to subject a territory and people to two separate and
independent governments without one of them becoming subordinate to, and the instrument of, the other.
And I am satisfied that the political leaders of the

[1] As to the absurdities taught under the doctrine of political sovereignty, see *post.* Chapter IX. on " State Sovereignty and the Right
of Secession."

day, such as Hamilton, Madison, and Randolph, who made such strenuous efforts to establish a strong federal government, put no faith in the feasibility of a dual government of this sort. For, upon the assembling of the constitutional convention, these statesmen advocated the establishment of a supreme federal government, which would reduce the States to subordinate provinces ; and they did not yield to the demands of the advocates of State rights until it was demonstrated that the convention would not adopt a centralized government. They feared, and the struggles of seventy-five years justified their fears, that the two governmental agencies could not maintain their independent autonomy. But against their will and in spite of their fears this became the fundamental principle of the American governmental agencies, about which the political forces played with more or less vehemence for three quarters of a century, until, as a declaration of the results of the mighty crisis, the Supreme Court of the United States pronounced this country to be " an indestructible Union composed of indestructible States." [1]

---

[1] " But the perpetuity and indissolubility of the Union by no means implies the loss of distinct and individual existence, or of the right of self-government by the States. Without the States in union there could be no such political body as the United States. (Lane County *v.* Oregon, 7 Wall., 71, 76.) Not only, therefore, can there be no loss of separate and independent autonomy to the States, through their union under the Constitution, but it may not unreasonably be said that the preservation of the States and the maintenance of their

It was the adoption of this principle which changed the Federal Union from a league to a composite state; or, to go to the German for apt expressions, from a *Staatenbund* to a *Bundestaat*, from a union of States to a state founded by the union of States.[1]

In the constitutional convention of 1787, every complexion of political thought was represented; and while, with the exception of a few irreconcilables, the entire convention felt the need of some radical change in the form or powers of the Federal Government, they were by no means agreed as to the proper measures for reform. They had assembled under instructions from Congress for the purpose of *revising* the Articles of Confederation, and hence they were not authorized to make any organic change in the character of the National Government. But having assembled in convention, and placed themselves under a pledge to keep the deliberations of the convention secret, until the new government had become firmly established, the Virginia delegation, aided by Hamilton, Wilson, and others, declared themselves boldly in favor of the revolutionary step of proposing an organic change in the form of gov-

---

governments are as much within the design and care of the Constitution as the preservation of the Union and the maintenance of the national government. The Constitution in all its provisions looks to an indestructible Union composed of indestructible States."—Chase, Ch.-J., in Texas *v.* White, 7 Wall. 700, 725.

[1] See *post.* Chapter IX. on "State Sovereignty and the Right of Secession."

ernment; and they pointed, as a justification of their extreme action, to the impotence of the Federal Government as long as its fundamental character remained unchanged. The Virginia plan of government was then introduced, which provided for a bicameral congress, both houses of which were to represent the people of the United States at large instead of the States. Under this plan of government Congress was not only to have the right to command directly the obedience of individuals, but also to exercise a negative upon all State legislation, by declaring what State legislation was constitutional. The adoption of this plan would have thrown the Federal Government completely into the control of the larger States. It is not surprising that the smaller States opposed its adoption and offered a substitute, known as the New Jersey plan, which consisted only of a revision of the existing articles by giving to Congress the power to regulate foreign and domestic commerce, to levy duties on imports, and to raise revenue by means of a stamp act. By the presentation of these two plans, the opposing parties were brought face to face, and their contentions for the mastery came near causing a disbanding of the convention. It is very likely, too, that the convention would have adjourned without having accomplished any thing, had not the urgent necessities of the political situa-

tion compelled some action. It will not be necessary to give in this place any minute account of
the contests between these opposing forces. Suffice
it to say that a compromise was effected, by giving
equal representation to the States in the Senate,
while the representatives were to be apportioned
according to population, the Senate representing
the States, while the House of Representatives
represented the people at large.

Other compromises followed, but wherever there
was no contest, the English precedents were followed, as in the formation of the State governments,
so that the President of the United States, like the
governors of the States, was an imitation of George
III., with the elective principle substituted for the
hereditary; while the Senate corresponded to the
House of Lords, and the House of Representatives
to the House of Commons.

It is certainly not necessary to go into detail
in order to prove that in the main the American
constitutions are an evolutionary growth out of the
British Constitution. There are, however, several
principles developed and brought into play by the
struggles for national life, which are not traceable to
the British Constitution, at least, not in the shape in
which they were made to operate in this country.
I have already alluded to the development of the
new form of federal government. That certainly

finds no parallel in British history. Another new principle, which first found expression in American politics, and which even now to some extent escapes the comprehension of European jurists, is that all governmental agencies are the creatures of the will of the people, and are subject to limitations imposed upon them by the popular will. Parliament is legally supreme, and so is every European government, whether it be republican or monarchical. No act of such governments can be unconstitutional in the American sense, for these governments have the power to change the constitutions at will. But inasmuch as in the United States the people themselves ordained and established their constitutions, and they alone can alter and amend them, any act of the legislatures or of Congress, which transcends the provisions of the Constitution, would be unconstitutional and void. This is the fundamental doctrine of American constitutional law, and it is only feasible where there is a written constitution containing explicit grants or limitations of power. But while this principle is not to be found in the constitutional law of any other country, it must not be inferred that it was a spontaneous creation. The American mind was undoubtedly prepared for the development of the principle by the fact, that all, or almost all, the colonial governments had been established under written charters, in which the powers of the colonial governments were more or less explicitly set forth. If the colonial government transcended these powers, the act was void, and could not have the force of law. The residuum of power was held to be in the British Crown. When the thirteen colonies were declared to be free and independent States, this residuum had to be lodged somewhere, and, of course, in accordance with the political philosophy of the French schools, which at that time had already obtained a strong hold upon the American mind, it was held to be reserved to the people. The people were thus held to be the masters, while the officials were the servants, who could only lawfully do the bidding of the people.. It is in this way that the fundamental doctrine of American democracy became established.

The third new principle developed in the American constitutional law was the power of the courts to declare an act of the legislature void which contravened a provision of the Constitution. But this principle is only a consequence of the principle that all governmental agencies are the servants of the people, who can exercise only those powers which are conceded to them by the written power of attorney. The courts are obliged to construe and determine the law, whenever a question is raised before them by parties litigant, and, being the servant of the people, they must obey the Constitution rather than an act of the legislature which violates the Constitution. For such an act of the legislature is not law. It being the duty of the courts to declare what is the law, they are obliged to determine when legislative acts are constitutional or unconstitutional. The colonial courts were habitually exercising this power, and the novelty in its exercise by the courts after the recognition of the independence of the States consists simply of the fact that there was then no foreign or superior government whose commands were obeyed in refusing to give effect to the legislation of the inferior government. The charters of government were then enacted by the people, instead of by a superior government.

A summary account has thus been given of the development of the American constitutions, Federal and State, and while there has been a rigorous exclusion from the narrative of the details which can be obtained in any respectable history of those times, I believe no serious objection would now be raised to the claim that the constitutional law of the United States, at least up to the adoption of the written constitutions, was developed along the same lines, as has been shown by the preceding chapter to be the case with law in general, viz., ' that the constitutional law was the resultant of all the social and other forces, which went to make up the civilization of the people. No serious difficulty in proving this part of the proposition was anticipated. But when the claim is made that the establishment of written constitutions has not materially altered the law of constitutional development, that American constitutional law follows and registers all material changes in public opinion, as unerringly as the needle follows the magnetic meridian, we are prepared for a most vigorous opposition. The commonly accepted doctrine is that unwritten constitutions, like the British Constitution, reflect accurately and promptly the mutations of public opinion, for Parliament, being subject to no legal limitations, with its hand constantly on the public pulse, in every case of permanent and effective legislation, simply records the decree of the people ; and if that decree involves the adoption of a new fundamental principle, a change is thus wrought in the British Constitution. But since the American constitutions are written and are established by a higher power, as a limitation of the powers of government, it is impossible for any changes in the Constitution to be made lawfully, except by the power which created the Constitution, viz., the people of the United States, or of the States, respectively. Recognizing the necessity for changes in constitutional law, in order that it may conform to the changes in popular opinion and public wants,

the framers of the constitutions have, in each case,
provided for the adoption of amendments. This is
generally accepted as the only way in which American constitutions may be changed.

If the entire constitutional law of the American
system of government had been reduced to writing,
and incorporated into one instrument, the fundamental obligation of obedience to the written word,
which is required by public opinion in every system
of jurisprudence,[1] until the power which enacted it
had repealed it, would bring about a practical prohibition of any change in the Constitution, except in
the prescribed way of amendment. And it is because the State constitutions enter more or less into
the details of constitutional law, that constitutional
conventions are called more or less frequently for
the purpose of revision. A convention has never
been called for the revision of the Federal Constitution; and the probability is that there never will
be, as long as this government remains Federal
and Republican. For if such a necessity would
be likely to arise, it would have arisen as a result
of the great contest of opposing forces, which was
settled finally and forever by the surrender at Appo-
mattox. If the Federal Constitution had consisted of any thing more than the skeleton of constitutional law, the same necessity for constitutional

---

[1] See the discussion on this point in the preceding chapter.

conventions would have been felt, as has been experienced in respect to the State constitutions. For
it is a demonstrated fact that the fragility and insta-
bility of a constitution are in direct proportion to
the multiplicity of its written rules. It is for the
reason that the Federal Constitution contains only
a declaration of the fundamental and most general
principles of constitutional law, while the real, living
constitutional law,—that which the people are made
to feel around and about them, controlling the exercise of power by government, and protecting the
minority from the tyranny of the majority—the
flesh and blood of the Constitution, instead of its
skeleton, is here, as well as elsewhere, unwritten ;
not to be found in the instrument promulgated by
a constitutional convention, but in the decisions
of the courts and acts of the legislature, which are
published and enacted in the enforcement of the
written Constitution. The unwritten constitution
of the United States, within the broad limitations of
the written Constitution, is just as flexible, and
yields just as readily to the mutations of public
opinion as the unwritten constitution of Great
Britain. But the opponents of this theory would
doubtless claim that the saving clause—*within the
broad limitations of the written Constitution*—de-
prives the theory of its value. That, however, is
only a superficial appearance. For, if by judicial

interpretation, in obedience to the stress of public opinion or private interests, the express limitations of the written Constitution are made to mean one thing at one time, and at another time an altogether different thing, there is very little restraint imposed by these written limitations. The only obstacle in the way of an untrammelled popular will is the bald letter of the Constitution ; and even that does not chain the popular will in times of great excitement and extreme necessity.[1] This is what is meant and what has been attained by the doctrine of the implied grant of powers, which was elaborated by Chief-Justice Marshall, and without which the Federal Constitution would not have lasted a half-century.

Mr. Jefferson was right when he said that John Marshall and the Supreme Court were engaged in making a constitution for the government. And the Supreme Court has continued to make constitutional law ever since. It is, no doubt, convenient for the practical lawyer to accept the fiction that the judge does not make law ; that he simply declares what was the pre-existing law ; but the critical student of political science repudiates it in the presence of the undoubted formulation by the courts of principles, never before enunciated, and which in many cases conflict hopelessly with the fundamental principles

---

[1] See *post.*, Chapter VII., The Constitution in the War of Secession.

of the past. No, the great body of American constitutional law cannot be found in the written in-
struments, which we call our constitutions ; it is
unwritten, in the constitutional and legal acceptation
of the term, and is to be found in the decisions of the
courts and the acts of the National and State legislatures, constantly changing with the demands of the
popular will.   These mutations are not so notable or
so striking in the constitutional law of the States, as
in that of the United States, nor are they so frequent ; but the difference is only in degree, and is to
be accounted for on the ground, that the State constitutions are not so elementary as the Federal
Constitution, and are therefore more inflexible, and
hence require frequent revisions by constitutional
convention.

In the succeeding pages, I will give striking examples of the mutations of constitutional law, which
will, I think, incontestably prove the correctness of
my thesis ; and, after proving that the changes do
occur, I will attempt to give a logical and ethical
justification of the fact.

CHAPTER III.

As a consequence of the struggles of the State-rights and National parties, in the convention of 1787, the selection of a President was provided for on a very unique plan. In order to keep the executive separate from and independent of the other departments of the government, some method had to be adopted, whereby his election could be had without the instrumentality of Congress. In order to satisfy the National party, the principle of popular representation had to be recognized, while State lines could not be ignored without causing dissatisfaction among the adherents of State sovereignty ; and there was entire unanimity among the delegates of all shades of political thought that the President and Vice-President should be selected free from party strife, so that they could faithfully represent the people, irrespective of party ties and party policies. To meet every demand, the convention devised the plan of election by electors chosen by the States, each State to choose as many electors as it had senators

46

and representatives in Congress. These electors were required to meet in their respective States to cast their votes for the men whom they considered best fitted to assume the responsible duties of these offices. These votes, sealed up, were to be transmitted to Congress, and to be opened by the President of the Senate and counted in the presence of the two Houses assembled in joint session. Provision was made for election by the Houses of Congress, the President by the House of Representatives, and the Vice-President by the Senate, in case no one received a majority of all the votes cast.

One great object, held in view in the adoption of this artificial system of election, was to remove the selection of the President as far away from the people as it was possible. Not only was that object manifest by the adoption of the plan itself, but it was to be observed by the manner of selecting the electors, viz., by the State legislatures, which at first generally prevailed. In the first two elections, there was no party strife, for no one appeared as a candidate for the Presidency in opposition to the man who was *facile princeps* among his countrymen. But even in the second election, in respect to the Vice-Presidency, party influence began to be felt in the actions of the electoral college. The electors who leaned to the Federal party were expected to vote for John Adams, while the anti-Federalists were expected

to vote for George Clinton. But in the third election, party strife was fully developed ; and although
no pledge was exacted of the electors, party influence was sufficiently strong to compel most of the
electors to vote for the leaders of their respective
parties, John Adams and Thomas Jefferson. By the
time that the fourth election was held, party organizations were perfected ; each party put up its candidates for President and Vice-President before the
selection of the electors, and the contest was not
over the electors so much as it was over the respective candidates for President and Vice-President,
which the two parties had nominated. Quietly and
as a matter of course, apparently, the discretion of
the electors, in the performance of their duty, van-
ished in the air, and ever since, the electors, who,
according to the spirit of the constitutional provision,
were expected to exercise a wise discretion in the
selection of a President and Vice-President, and who
were first selected, and were intended by the framers
of the Constitution to be selected, for their superior
wisdom and knowledge of the merits and qualifications of our public men, are called on to simply
register the decree of the nominating convention of
the party which was successful at the polls. The
contest is at an end, when the election for electors is
over. It is not necessary to wait for the meeting of
the electors in order to learn who would be the next

President and Vice-President. Public opinion is so strong against the exercise of discretion by an elector, that if one should be rash enough to exercise the discretion, which the spirit of the written Constitution requires him to exercise, he would be buried under a public obloquy, that would be without limit, for he would be considered guilty of a treachery to his party, that would find condonation nowhere.

Now what is the real, living constitutional rule as to the selection of a President and Vice-President? that they are to be selected after deliberation by the electors, as being the men whom the electors considered best fitted to fill the positions; or that they must be nominated by parties, and selected by a popular election, indirectly through the choice of the electors of one party or of the other? There can be no hesitation in coming to the conclusion that the latter is the real, living constitutional rule.

But it must not be supposed that the written constitutional rule has been altogether deprived of its influence upon popular action. Following the fundamental rule, which requires obedience to the written word, until the power which enacted it has repealed it, the popular selection of President and Vice-President is still required to be made indirectly through the election of presidential electors. And there is no better illustration of the doctrine that constitutional law is the resultant of *all* the forces

3

at play in society than to point out some of the surprising and unforeseen consequences of the existing system of election of these officers. The method of selecting the electors was soon changed to the popular election at the polls, and the entire number of electors, to which a State is entitled, are now voted for by the State at large. Consequently, when the popular decree in any State is delivered in favor of one party or of the other, all the chosen electors of that State will be cast for the presidential nominees of the succcessful party, it matters not how large or how small the majority may have been. In consequence of the variance in the size of the majorities of the different States, it has very frequently happened that the candidates who are elected received only a minority of the votes cast in the popular election. Thus has been prevented a full realization of the demand for a popular election of presidential candidates.

CHAPTER IV.

THE RE-ELIGIBILITY OF THE PRESIDENT.

THE written Constitution of the United States does not prescribe any limit to the re-eligibility of the President. But Washington in his Farewell Address at the close of his second term announced his determination to decline re-election, on the ground that the safety of republican institutions demanded the imposition of a limit to the President's re-eligibility ; and that in his judgment the limit ought to be placed at two terms of office. The popular regrets on his retirement from public life were mingled with hearty approval of the patriotic reasons he assigned for his action. Of the Presidents who were re-elected, down to General Grant, Jefferson, Madison, Monroe, and Jackson survived the expiration of their second term, and, in obedience to the exalted precedent of Washington, retired from the political field. Their names were not proposed for re-election even by their most enthusiastic friends and admirers. Mr. Lincoln was re-elected, but was assassinated during his second term.

General Grant was elected to the presidency in 1868, and again in 1872. His great personal popularity, notwithstanding the dissatisfaction with his executive career, created a demand on the part of his friends for a third election. Soundings were taken of public opinion on the subject, and the opposition to his re-election, on the general principle enunciated by Washington, was so manifest from the utterances of the press, that his candidacy was abandoned in 1876, and Mr. Hayes became the Republican nominee and ultimately the President. But in 1880, towards the close of Mr. Hayes' administration, the friends of General Grant pressed his claims for a re-nomination, and urged that the spirit of the precedent set by Washington would not be violated by the re-nomination of Grant in 1880, since he would not be succeeding himself. His supporters in the National Republican Convention numbered 306, while the remainder of the delegates, constituting the majority, were divided among a number of strong candidates. After a prolonged contest, Mr. Garfield was nominated, as the compromise candidate of those who opposed the re-nomination of General Grant. This second repulse of the attempt to re-nominate and re-elect Grant is accepted as a final decision of the people that no man, however distinguished or popular, shall hold more than two terms of the presidency. For, although this condemnation was not received at the polls, every one is satisfied that the opposition to a third term was stronger outside of the Republican party, than it was within that party ; and even if Grant had received the third nomination at the hands of his party, he would have without doubt been overwhelmingly defeated at the polls.

Of course this popular decision cannot be taken as pronouncing the election to the presidency for a third term to be unconstitutional, in the sense that if one should be elected for a third term, he could be prevented from holding the office and exercising the duties thereof, on the ground that he was not lawfully elected to the office. For his election for a third term would have to be taken as a repeal of the constitutional rule previously enunciated. But if the object of constitutional law is to impose limitations upon the people and upon governmental agencies, surely the popular limitation upon the re-eligibility of the President can be taken as a constitutional limitation ; to be sure, not to be found in the written Constitution, but in that unwritten constitution, whose flexible rules reflect all the changes in public opinion. This is an example of a limitation of the unwritten constitution, which finds no authority whatever in the written Constitution, and yet as long as public opinion does not undergo a change, it is as binding as any written limitation, and even more binding than some of the plainest directions of the written Constitution.

CHAPTER V.

THE INVIOLABILITY OF CORPORATE CHARTERS AND
OF CHARTER RIGHTS.

IN Art. I., sec. 10, of the Constitution, it is provided that "no State shall pass any law . . . impairing the obligation of a contract."

The history of the times reveals a strong and very general disposition towards repudiation of debts, prompted without doubt by the sense of prostration under the heavy load of indebtedness fastened upon the people as a consequence of their contest with England. In order to prevent such repudiation, this clause was inserted in the Federal Constitution. I do not believe that any one would claim for this clause any other object than the prevention of repudiation of public and private debts by State legislation. Hence, if the intention of the framers of the Constitution is to furnish the true construction, we must conclude that nothing would be included within the operation of this prohibition but debts and other obligations issuing out of contracts.

But when the Supreme Court of the United States was called upon, in the determination of the power of the New Hampshire legislature, by an amendment to its charter, to change the composition of the Board of Trustees of Dartmouth College, to construe the meaning and effect of this clause, it was held, under the lead of Chief-Justice Marshall, who delivered the opinion of the court, that the charter of incorporation of a private corporation was a contract which could not be impaired or altered by subsequent legislation, unless the power of amendment was reserved; and that the act of the legislature of New Hampshire, creating a new college corporation, and directing a transfer to them of the control of Dartmouth College and of its property, was such an impairment of the obligation of a contract as to be void under this clause of the Federal Constitution.[1]

Under the influence of the decision of the court in the Dartmouth College case, it has been held that subsequent legislatures are bound by legislative con-

---

[1] "It can require no argument to prove that the circumstances of this case constitute a contract. An application is made to the crown for a charter to incorporate a religious and literary institution. In the application it is stated that large contributions have been made for the object, which will be conferred on the corporation as soon as it shall be created. The charter is granted, and on its faith the property is conveyed. Surely, in this transaction, every ingredient of a complete and legitimate contract is to be found."—Marshall, Ch. J., in Dartmouth College Case *v.* Woodward, 4 Wheat., 518, 627.

tracts to exempt persons and corporations from liability for taxes. The decisions in support of this proposition are to be found in great numbers, both in the State and Federal reports. It suffices to refer here to only a few decisions of the Supreme Court of the United States, in which we first find intima- tion in the dissenting opinions of the future modifi- cation of the ruling in the Dartmouth College and other early cases.[1] In these decisions, the opinion of the majority of the court seems to go the length of holding to the inviolability of any contract made by a legislature which was not prohibited by the Constitution, even though its performance would be injurious to the commonwealth; while the dissent- ing opinions rest their objections to the decision of the court on the ground that the power of taxation was political, and that the legislature cannot barter away it or any other political power.

But it was not long before the injurious effect of the decision of the Dartmouth College case was ap- preciated, and it became an almost universal legisla- tive custom to grant charters subject to repeal and amendment. But that custom did not prevent the decision from working a dangerous effect in recog-

---

[1] State Bank of Ohio *v.* Knoop, 16 How., 376; Ohio Life Ins. and Trust Co. *v.* Debolt, 16 How., 376.

See, to the same effect, Billings *v.* Providence Bank, 4 Pet., 514; Gordon *v.* Appeal Tax Court, 3 How., 133; Home of the Friendless *v.* Rowse; Washington University *v.* Rowse, 8 Wall., 430, 439.

nizing the inviolability of charter privileges. The dangerous consequences of this doctrine were exemplified by the facts of the case of Charles River Bridge Company *v.* Warren River Bridge Company, 11 Pet., 536. The Charles River Bridge Company had been authorized to establish and maintain a bridge across the Charles River, and to charge toll for its use for a stated period, at the lapse of which the bridge was to become public. This bridge was constructed in pursuance of this grant, and after it had been in use for some time, but before the expiration of the period for which the Charles River Bridge Company had been granted the right to charge toll, the legislature authorized the construction of a second bridge, connecting the same places, and situated within a short distance of the first bridge. It is plain that the construction of the second bridge could under those circumstances have had but one effect upon the franchise of the Charles River Bridge Company—viz., an immediate serious diminution in the profits of that company, and an ultimate destruction of the franchise in consequence of the second bridge being opened to the public without charge at an earlier day. It had already become public when the decision in the case was pronounced by the Supreme Court of the United States. The public pressure in favor of the second bridge was so great that, notwithstanding it was a plain case of impairment of the charter rights of the Charles River Bridge Company, the court, under the lead of Chief-Justice Taney, gave judgment for the Warren River Bridge Company, resting its decision on the technical ground that all grants of the State must be construed favorably to the State, and strictly against the grantee; that the grant of a franchise will not be considered as an exclusive monopoly, unless expressly declared to be so, and that the incidental injury proceeding from the grant of a second franchise would not be, in the constitutional sense, an impairment of the obligation of a contract. Public opinion was not yet ripe for an open repudiation of the doctrine of the Dartmouth College case; and hence the end was attained by the employment of a technicality.[1]

But from this time to the present the power of private corporations has increased rapidly, every advance in science and industry tending to develop the proportions and the strength of corporations, until there is a general popular fear of an usurpation by them of control of the government. The popular demand for a control of railroad and other corporations became so great and so urgent, that it was impossible for Congress or the courts to ignore it. Laws

---

[1] Charles River Bridge Co. *v.* Warren River Bridge Co., 11 Pet., 536. See, to same effect, Richmond R.R. Co. *v.* Louisa. R.R. Co., 13 How., 71.

were passed subjecting railroads to all sorts of regulations, and finally they were placed in many States under the control of a railroad commission. On the general principles, that corporations, like natural persons, were subject to the police power of the State, and that there was no impairment of the obligation of a contract, if a railroad corporation were subjected to reasonable special police regulations, although these regulations increased the liabilities of the corporations and diminished their income, it was held that this police power could not be bartered away by the legislature.[1] And so, also, has it been held that there is no violation of the constitutional prohibition of impairment of the obligation of a contract where corporations are subjected to a regulation of their charges by State officers or commissions. This was held to be only one phase of the police power of the State, and that the charters were issued subject to the exercise of the power.[2]

So far in the course of this constitutional development, it has been possible for the courts, by the aid of technicalities and refinements of verbal meanings,

---

[1] Thorpe *v.* Rutland, 27 Vt., 140; Railroad Co. *v.* Fuller, 17 Wall., 560; Chicago, etc., R.R. Co. *v.* Haggerty, 67 Ill., 113; Haas *v.* Railroad Co., 141 Wis., 44; Pennsylvania R.R. Co. *v.* Lewis, 79 Pa. St., 33.

[2] Chicago, etc., R.R. Co. *v.* Iowa, 94 U. S., 115; Peck *v.* Chicago, etc., R.R. Co., 94 U. S., 164, 176; Union Pac. Ry. *v.* United States, 99 U. S., 700.

to claim that there has been no repudiation of the Dartmouth College case. It is true that there is not the slightest hint, in the opinion of Chief-Justice Marshall, of the subjection of the corporate rights to an indefinable and elastic power, called police power, in the exercise of which it is possible for the interests of the corporation to be jeopardized. But that can be explained away by holding that the facts of the Dartmouth College case did not require any acknowledgment of the police power of the government. There are, however, two later cases, which cannot be substantially reconciled with the position of the court in the Dartmouth College case. I refer to the cases of Stone *v.* Mississippi, 101 U. S., 814, and Fertilizing Co. *v.* Hyde Park, 97 U. S., 659. In the first case, Stone *v.* Mississippi, the question arose on a repeal of the charter of a lottery company by a 'new provision of the State constitution. The court held that the abolition of the lottery company was nothing more than the exercise of the police power, and did not offend the constitutional provision under discussion. After maintaining that " the doctrines of Trustees of Dartmouth College *v.* Woodward (4 Wheat., 518), announced by this court more than sixty years ago, have become so imbedded in the jurisprudence of the United States, as to make them to all intents and purposes a part of the Constitution itself," Chief-Justice Waite proceeds:

"The contracts which the Constitution protects are those that relate to property rights, not governmental. It is not always easy to tell on which side of the line which separates governmental from property rights a particular case is to be put, but in respect to lotteries there can be no difficulty. They are not, in the legal acceptation of the term *mala in se*, but, as we have just seen, may properly be made *mala prohibita*. They are a species of gambling, and wrong in their influences. They disturb the checks and balances of a well-ordered community. Society built on such a foundation would almost of necessity bring forth a population of speculators and gamblers, living on the expectation of what 'by the casting of lots, or by lot, chance or otherwise,' might be 'awarded' to them from the accumulation of others. Certainly the right to suppress them is governmental, to be exercised at all times by those in power, at their discretion. Any one, therefore, who accepts a lottery charter does so with the implied understanding that the people, in their sovereign capacity, and through their properly constituted agencies, may resume it at any time when the public good shall require, whether it be paid for or not. All that one can get by such a charter is a suspension of certain governmental rights in his favor, subject to withdrawal at will. He has in legal effect nothing more than a license to enjoy the privilege on the terms named for the specified time, unless it be sooner abrogated by the sovereign power of the State. It is a permit, good as against existing laws, but subject to future legislative and constitutional control or withdrawal." [1]

In answer to the criticism that the rulings of the court, that legislative contracts of exemptions from taxation are inviolable by subsequent legislatures, would require the court to pronounce this action of the Mississippi Constitutional Convention to be unconstitutional, the Chief-Justice says:

"We have held, not however without strong opposition at times, that this clause protected a corporation in its charter exemptions from taxation. While taxation is in general necessary for the support of government, it is not part of the government itself. Govern-

[1] Stone *v.* Mississippi, 101 U. S., 820, 821.

ment was not organized for the purposes of taxation, but taxation may be necessary for the purposes of government. As such, taxation becomes an incident to the exercise of the legitimate functions of government, but nothing more. No government dependent on taxation for support can bargain away its whole power of taxation, for that would be substantial abdication. All that has been determined thus far is, that for a consideration it may, in the exercise of a reasonable discretion, and for the public good, surrender a part of its powers in this particular." [1]

In the case of the Fertilizing Company *v.* Hyde Park,[2] the facts were these: The plaintiff corporation was granted the privilege of establishing a factory for the conversion of offal into fertilizers within a certain district in the vicinity of Chicago; and that this privilege should be enjoyed undisturbed for fifty years. The city of Hyde Park sprang up around the fertilizing factory, after the manner of western towns, and of course the inhabitants complained of the factory as a nuisance. The legislature of Illinois directed the closing up or removal of the factory within two years. This legislative action was taken before the expiration of the period for which the privilege of maintaining the factory in that locality had been granted. On an appeal to the courts it was finally determined by the Supreme Court of the United States, that this legislative prohibition of the continuance of the factory in the same place was not an im-

[1] Stone *v.* Miss., 101, W. S. 820 ; Ch.-J. Waite.
[2] 97 U. S., 659.

pairment of the obligation of the contract created by the grant of the privilege, since it was but the ordinary exercise of police-power, subject to which all legislative grants are made. Mr. Justice Miller concurred in the judgment on the ground that the legislature could compel the removal of the factory to a less objectionable location, since the contract of the legislature with the company did not specify any particular location in which to establish the factory. But the Justice took exception to the position taken by the majority of the court in the opinion of Justice Swayne, saying:

" It is said that such contract as may be found in the present case was made subject to the police power of the legislature over the class of subjects to which it relates. The extent to which this is true depends upon the specific character of the contract and not upon the general doctrine. This court has repeatedly decided that a State may by contract bargain away her right of taxation. I have not concurred in that view, but it is the settled law of this court. If a State may make a contract on that subject which it cannot abrogate or repeal, it may, with far more reason, make a contract for a limited time for the removal of a continuing nuisance from a populous city.

" The nuisance in the case before us was the very subject-matter of the contract. The consideration of the contract was that the company might and should do certain things which affected the health and comfort of the community ; and the State can no more impair the obligation of that contract than it can resume the right of taxation which it has on valid consideration agreed not to exercise, because in either case the wisdom of its legislation has become doubtful.

" If the good of the entire community requires the destruction of the company's rights under this contract, let the entire community pay therefore by condemning the same for public use." [1]

[1] Pp. 670, 671.

Mr. Justice Strong dissented from the judgment of the court, criticising the ground taken by Mr. Justice Miller as well as that taken by the majority of the court :

" It has been suggested that the charter did not precisely designate the place where the rendering works might be established, and to which the city offal might be carried ; and hence it is argued that, notwithstanding the contract, it is within the power of the legislature to order the removal of the works to another locality, and that this may be done mediately by the municipal corporation empowered by the State. The inference I emphatically deny. It is true the charter empowered the company to select a location within certain geographical limits, and did not itself define the exact point ; but when under this power a location was made by the company and hundreds of thousands of dollars were expended upon it, it was beyond the power of the other contracting party to change it. The location was lawful when made, and if lawful then, it cannot be unlawful afterwards. . . . It must be, therefore, that the location of the company's works at the places where they were located, recognized as a proper location by the act of the legislature of 1869, is one which cannot be changed without the consent of both parties to the contract." [1]

" That the charter granted by the legislature, March 8, 1867, and accepted by the company, is a contract protected by the Constitution of the United States, cannot be denied, in the face of the Dartmouth College *v.* Woodward (4 Wheat., 518), and the long line of decisions that have followed in its wake and reasserted its doctrines. And if the company holds its rights under and by force of the contract, those rights cannot be taken away or impaired, either directly or indirectly, by any subsequent legislation." [2]

It has also been held by the same court that there is no impairment of the obligation of the contract made with a brewing or distilling corporation, that

---

[1] Page 677.
[2] Strong, J., p. 672.

its business is subsequently destroyed, and its property rendered valueless, by a general prohibition of the manufacture and sale of intoxicating liquors.[1]

It is impossible for one to read between the lines of these decisions, and to compare the facts of the cases, without reaching the conclusion that there has been a decided shifting of the position of the court since the case of Dartmouth College *v.* Woodward. In that case, the Supreme Court prohibited a simple change in the personnel of the college board of trustees, although this change would not deprive the real beneficiaries, the students, of any advantage derivable under the old charter. In these later decisions, the court has permitted the practical destruction of corporate property and privileges, guaranteed by legislative grant, on the ground that corporations, as well as natural persons, are subject to the control of the police power of the State. The welfare of the communities required these interferences with property and franchises, since their enjoyment threatened or actually inflicted evil. But the same reason might have been urged in favor of the New Hampshire interference with Dartmouth College. Nowhere can one man exert a more powerful influence over the minds and hearts of others than in the professor's chair. The legislature may have had reason to fear that

---

[1] Beer Company *v.* Massachusetts, 97 U. S., 25 ; Mugler *v.* Kansas, 123 U. S., 623 ; Powell *v.* Pennsylvania, 127 U. S., 678.

5

the presence of so many tory representatives on the old board of trustees of the college would exert a baneful influence upon the minds of the youths who would attend the college. If they truly thought this danger was imminent, they would have been justified in stamping this evil out of existence. Other nations have for the same reason banished a hostile population, or expropriated their land.

The facts of these cases do not vary materially : the difference in the opinions cannot be accounted for on this ground. The contradiction arises out of a change in public opinion, and a consequent change in the constitutional rule. Nothing but a profound respect and reverence for the great Chief-Justice who penned the decision in the Dartmouth College case has compelled this show of indorsement of its principles in the later decisions of the Supreme Court, while the rule is substantially modified, if not abrogated altogether.

CHAPTER VI.

THE DOCTRINE OF NATURAL RIGHTS IN AMERICAN CONSTITUTIONAL LAW.

PERHAPS no product of the Roman law has exerted so potent an influence upon the development of modern jurisprudence as the Roman doctrine of *jus naturale.* When Rome was in its infancy, the national dominion was in its character personal, and not territorial; *i.e.*, the governmental power was exerted over the individuals who composed the Roman people, and not over the country which they occupied. The tie of nationality bound the Romans to each other, and not to the land; hence the early Roman law did not take into consideration strangers who might be resident within the Roman territory. The *jus civile*, the name given to the early Roman law, was designed to determine the legal relations and rights of Roman citizens only, and did not take cognizance even of the claims of Roman citizens against these resident strangers. The stranger had no right which the Roman was obliged to respect, nor was he under any obligations to the Romans with whom he may have had dealings. But this anomalous state of affairs could not last long. With the increase of Rome's international intercourse, the demand for rules of law, which could apply to transactions with foreigners, became greater and greater until, finally, the Roman government provided a special judge for the hearing of all causes of actions arising between strangers and between strangers and Romans. The *jus civile*, like the beginnings of all systems of jurisprudence, was extremely technical and symbolical; and to apply this law in all its strictness to the adjudication of the rights of strangers, who could not be presumed to know any thing of this law, would have resulted often in the infliction of wrong, rather than the dispensation of justice. Instead of deciding these causes of action according to the *jus civile*, the Roman prætor, who was given charge of them, rendered his decisions in accordance with those rules of law which obtained generally among all nations. The law, thus developed alongside of the *jus civile*, became known as the *jus gentium*, or the law of nations.

On account of the general and almost universal character of its rules of conduct, the *jus gentium* became much less technical and more rational than the *jus civile ;* and when the time arrived for the transformation of Roman law from its crude empirical character into a science, the *jus gentium* was found to be of far greater importance than the *jus civile*, although originally the former was intended to play a subordinate part in the development of the system.

About the same time the Roman lawyers, together with other serious and thoughtful men of the day, revolting from the prevalent profligacy, became infatuated with the stoic philosophy, and drew from that philosophy the Greek idea of natural law. Instead of the *jus gentium* being received as a body of rules found to be generally enforced by all nations, it became, in its reduction to the forms of a science, the *jus naturale*, an ideal law which one in his imagination would conceive to be in force in a state of perfect nature. *Jus naturale* is the scientific, idealized form of the *jus gentium*.

It is impossible for one to suppose that the accomplished Roman jurists really believed that by their labors they were taking the world back to the legal relations of the aboriginal peoples, who knew no state, no legislator, and who were supposed to have lived in a state of nature. It is conceivable that poets may imagine the perfection of legal relations under such a natural law ; but the hard common-sense of the Roman lawyer, would without doubt have revolted at the thought of finding the perfection of legal reasoning in the chaos which precedes organized national life. In the same way that these jurists yearned for a release of the world from its habits of profligacy and gross indulgence, by the adoption of simpler and more rational modes of living, so did they strive to strip the law of its barbarous and gross technicalities, and make it approximate the perfection of reason, by reducing it to the comparative simplicity of form, which one may well conceive to be the character of a natural law, enforced among the most rational, the most highly developed people. It was the simplicity of form, rather than the rational content of the law, as projected by them, and its development without the active interference of the state, which made them compare it with law in a state of nature.

But the cruder form of this doctrine obtained a stronghold upon the legal thought of the middle ages, and men really believed that we had fallen from a more glorious state of nature, and that were we able to retrace the steps taken in the progress of the world, we could regain that natural state, where law was the perfection of reason, and barbarous technicalities and injustice were unknown. The doctrine reaches the extreme limits of absurdity in the social contract, in the claim that all governmental authority, and hence the binding force of law, is derived from the agreement or consent of the governed; and that all men are possessed of certain natural rights, rights enjoyed by them in a state of

nature, and which no government can rightfully in-
fringe or take away. This doctrine of a social contract has dominated modern thought in a more or
less modified form to the present day, and even now
resists tenaciously the heavy onslaughts made upon
it by jurists of the Bentham-Austin school.

In the reaction from the all-powerful influence of
this doctrine of a social contract, and of absolute
natural rights, the pendulum of modern scientific
thought has swung too far in the opposite direction.
A large and influential school of English jurists,
whose chief apostles and expounders have been Bentham and Austin, repudiate entirely the Roman
doctrine of *jus naturale.* Defining law to be the
command of a sovereign to a subject, and recognizing
the will of the sovereign to be the only standard of
right, they push their doctrine to the extreme of
denying that the consideration of any so-called natural rights could properly fall within the province of
jurisprudence, and confining it strictly to the realm
of ethical questions.

Technically, this criticism of the Roman doctrine
jus naturale is sound ; for there can be no legal right
which is not recognized or created by the sovereign
power of the state. The commands of the sovereign are always law, and hence legally right, it
matters not how many so-called natural rights are
thereby violated. But the error of the Austinites,

in this case, as in the general question of the origin and development of law,[1] lies in failing to take note of the fact that popular notions of rights, however wrong they may be from a scientific standpoint, do become incorporated into, and exert an influence upon, the development of the actual law. Every legal principle is the resultant of some two or more social forces ; and popular notions are usually more powerful than physical facts. So far, therefore, as the doctrine of natural rights has moulded the principles of the law, a recognition of the doctrine will be necessary to a comprehension of the law ; and to that extent would a study of the doctrine of natural rights fall within the province of jurisprudence.

So far as the *jus naturale* of the Romans became a part of the existing Roman law, it belonged to the province of jurisprudence. The adoption and promulgation of its rules by the proper authorities simply indicated that they were habitually and spontaneously obeyed by the masses, and needed only to be enforced against the rebellious minority. But so far as the rules of the *jus naturale* did not meet with popular obedience, whose indorsement was advocated only by the more advanced thinkers, because they approximated their highest ethical conceptions, we must concede that the *jus naturale* has no place in the province of jurisprudence. When, therefore,

---

[1] See Chapter I.

a modern writer attacks an existing rule of law, on the ground that it offends the principles of natural law, or violates some natural right, the statement would have been the same if he said that the law was ethically indefensible.   In the province of jurisprudence there is, therefore, no room for the assertion of natural rights, except so far as they are recognized and protected by the existing law.   The same difference exists between natural rights and legal rights, as was recognized as existing between the morality of law and the morality of ethics.[1]

But even as a part of ethics, there is no fixed, invariable list of natural rights. These natural rights vary and their characters change with the development of the ethical conceptions of the people, the development of the legal rights keeping pace with, and following behind, the development of natural or ethical rights.   Indeed, the natural rights with which all men are proclaimed in the American Declaration of Independence to be endowed by their Creator, have been developed within the historical memory of man. Personal rights of all kinds were unknown in the dawn of history.   In all the Aryan races the individual was originally deemed to be possessed of no rights.   The family was the legal unit, and the patriarch, as the representative of the family, autocratically determined the fate and destiny of his

---

[1] See Chapter I.

wife, children, and slaves. His despotic will knew
no limits but those imposed by the softening influence of love. There was no legal or moral limit to
his power. Disobedience to the husband, father, or
master was declared to be the gravest crime, and
subjected the offender to the possible loss of his life.
As long as the patriarch lived the members of his
family remained under his power; when a woman
married she passed from the dominion of her family
patriarch to that of her husband's patriarch, and of
course the children of the marriage were under like
subjection. The patriarch also had the absolute
disposition of all the property acquired by the different members of the family.

A little later, a change in the law was demanded
by the prevalent sense of right, so far as to enable
sons, upon their arrival at a certain age, to acquire
an independent legal position, and to possess and
enjoy the rights of life, liberty, and property, free
from the interference of the father. But females of
all ages remained under the dominion of their
fathers until their marriage, when they passed under the dominion of their husbands. All persons
under age were held to be incapable of having any
independent legal rights.

Later on, single women were placed upon the same
footing with men, and married women and minors
were conceded independent rights of property; but

it was still considered a natural right for the father
to restrain and control the actions of his minor
child, and the husband those of his wife. This was
the condition of the law of domestic relations at the
beginning of the present century. Since then there
has been a gradual emancipation of the wife from
the control of the husband in this country, in the
more advanced States the married woman having
the same freedom from restraint as the single
woman. We are also on the eve of witnessing the
abrogation of the supposed natural right of the
parent to control the actions of his minor child, and
to educate it spiritually and intellectually as he
should see fit. Instead of recognizing in the parent
a *right* to exercise this control over the minor child,
the latest judicial opinion treats this control of the
child as a trust, reposed by the State in the parent
for the benefit of the child ; and that whenever the
State should determine that the trust is not being
properly executed, or that the public interests or
the interests of the child require the execution
of the trust by the State itself, there is no limit
to the power of the State to interfere with the
parental control. The confinement of minor children in reformatory schools, and compulsory education by the State, to the exclusion of private
education, can alone be justified by a denial of any
right in the parent to determine the destiny of his

child.' Thus we see, according to the earliest law of the Aryan races, the individual had no legal standing, and was the subject of no rights, unless he happened to be the head of a family. In this representative capacity, he was the autocratic possessor of all the rights of the family. At the present time, each individual stands free before the law, the independent possessor of his own rights, except when tender age or mental imbecility require him for his own good to be placed under tutelage.

There is, therefore, no such thing, even in ethics, as an absolute, inalienable, natural right. The so-called natural rights depend upon, and vary with, the legal and ethical conceptions of the people. As presently developed, the doctrine of natural rights may be tersely stated to be a freedom from all legal restraint that is not needed to prevent injury to others; a right to do any thing that does not involve a trespass or injury to others; or, to employ the language of Herbert Spencer: "Every man has freedom to do aught that he wills, provided he infringes not the equal freedom of any other man." The prohibitory operation of the law must be confined to the enforcement of the legal maxim, *sic utere tuo, ut alienum non lædas.* This right of

---

[1] See Tiedeman's "Limitations of Police Power," §§ 165, 166, 166a, 167.

[2] "Social Statics," p. 121.

freedom from needless restraint has been guaranteed
to the British subject by the Magna Charta, the
Petition of Right, and the Bill of Rights. And
while these several state papers, which in the main
constitute the English Constitution, are in fact acts
of Parliament, repealable by any Parliament, yet
their contents are so highly esteemed by public
opinion that they have been raised above ordinary
enactments, and practically operate to restrain the
power of Parliament. An act of Parliament, which
would flagrantly violate the fundamental principles
of the Magna Charta, could not be enforced, and
the political future of the party and persons responsible for its enactment would be irretrievably
damaged. But there is no binding force in the
prohibitions of the Magna Charta, except so far as
they are now voiced by public sentiment. The
solemn enactment of this celebrated statute undoubtedly does check the growth of public sentiment away from its principles; but if an act of
Parliament should be passed in accordance with
some great public demand, the fact that it violated
these principles would not prevent its enforcement
by the courts. Mr. Austin, therefore, is justified in
saying that English constitutional law belongs to
the province of ethics, and cannot be called a branch
of jurisprudence.

These same declarations of natural rights have

been incorporated into the American constitutions, both State and Federal. The Federal Constitution contains specific and general limitations upon the power of both State and Federal governments, while the State constitutions impose limitations upon the respective State governments. Most of the State constitutions also contain formal declarations, called Bills of Rights, enumerating somewhat in detail the rights of the citizen which the State government must respect. Thus the prevalent doctrine of natural rights was formulated and made a part of the organic law of the land, to be respected and enforced until repealed or changed by the proper authority. All the American constitutions make it the duty of the courts to prevent any violation of these rights by the other departments of the government by refusing to enforce laws which contain such violations of constitutional rights.

With the general growth and spread of popular government, there appeared a political philosophy whose central thought and fundamental maxim was, that society, collectively and individually, can attain, its highest development by being left free from governmental control, as far as this is possible, provision being made by the government only for the protection of the individual and of society by the punishment of crimes and trespasses. The so-called *laissez-faire* philosphy has, until lately, so controlled public opinion in the English-speaking world, that no disposition has been manifested by the depositaries of political power to do more than to control the criminal classes, provide for the care of the unfortunate poor and insane, and make public improvements. Hence in the early days of our national life, the discussions in constitutional law were chiefly confined to a consideration of the more formal provisions, which determined the methods of governmental procedure, and defined the limits of each branch of the government, the all-important question being the relative superiority of the National and State governments. In those days little was thought of those "glittering generalities," as they were called, which made it a part of our constitutional law that man is possessed of certain inalienable rights, that cannot be denied to him by government, and which denied to government the power to do more than to prevent the infliction of injuries upon others. These general declarations of private rights were not then considered as important in controlling the power of government, because the government manifested no disposition to violate them. But a change has since then come over the political thought of the country. Under the stress of economical relations, the clashing of private interests, the conflicts of labor and capital, the old superstition that government has the power to banish evil from the earth, if it could only be induced to declare the supposed causes illegal, has been revived; and all these so-called natural rights, which the framers of our constitutions declared to be inalienable, and the violation of which they pronounced to be a just cause for rebellion, are in imminent danger of serious infringement. The State is called on to protect the weak against the shrewdness of the stronger, to determine what wages a workman shall receive for his labor, and how many hours he shall labor. Many trades and occupations are being prohibited, because some are damaged incidentally by their prosecution, and many ordinary pursuits are made government monopolies. The demands of the Socialists and Communists vary in degree and in detail, but the most extreme of them insist upon the assumption by government of the paternal character altogether, abolishing all private property in land, and making the State the sole possessor of the working capital of the nation.

Contemplating these extraordinary demands of the great army of discontents, and their apparent power, with the growth and development of universal suffrage, to enforce their views of civil polity upon the civilized world, the conservative classes stand in constant fear of the advent of an absolutism more tyrannical and more unreasoning than any before experienced by man,—the absolutism of a democratic majority.

In these days of great social unrest, we applaud the disposition of the courts to seize hold of these general declarations of rights as an authority for them to lay their interdict upon all legislative acts which interfere with the individual's natural rights, even though these acts do not violate any specific or special provision of the Constitution. These general provisions furnish sufficient authority for judicial interference. As Judge Cooley [1] has forcibly said in respect to the regulation of trades and professions:

" What the legislature ordains and the constitution does not prohibit must be lawful. But if the constitution does no more than to provide that no person shall be deprived of his life, liberty, or property, except by due process of law, it makes an important provision on this subject, because it is an important part of civil liberty to have the right to follow all lawful employments."

The cases in which these general provisions of the Constitution have been declared by the courts to be binding upon the government, are numerous. At an early day, it was judicially decided in Massachusetts that slavery was abolished in that State by a provision of the State constitution, which declared that "all men are born free and equal, and have certain natural, essential, and inalienable rights," etc. [2]

/ Daily the courts are declaring acts of the legislature to be unconstitutional, because they violate pri-

---

[1] Cooley on Torts, p. 277.

[2] See Draper's "Civil War in America," vol. i., p. 317 ; Bancroft, "Hist. of U. S.," vol. x., p. 365 ; Cooley's "Principles of Const.," p. 213.

6

vate rights, guaranteed by no other provisions of the constitutions, but these general declarations of rights. To quote from a late decision of the New York Court of Appeals [1]:

" The main guaranty of private rights against unjust legislation is found in that memorable clause in the bill of rights, that no man shall be deprived of life, liberty, or property without due process of law. This guaranty is not construed in any narrow or technical sense. The right to life may be invaded without its destruction. One may be deprived of his liberty in a constitutional sense without putting his person in confinement. Property may be taken without manual interference therewith, or its physical destruction. The right to life includes the right of the individual to his body in its completeness and without dismemberment ; the right to liberty, the right to exercise his faculties, and to follow a lawful avocation for the support of life ; the right of property, the right to acquire property and enjoy it in any way consistent with the equal rights of others and the just exactions and demands of the State."

[1] Bertholf *v.* O'Reilly, 74 N. Y., 509.

CHAPTER VII.

IT is very common to hear that, in the effort to save the Union from dismemberment, the provisions of the Constitution for the protection of the individual against tyranny and oppression were set aside, and interferences with personal liberty were commonly practised, in violation of express provisions of the written Constitution. This charge is true in two important particulars. In the first place, the President, by his proclamation and without the consent of Congress, suspended the right to the writ of *habeas corpus*, and authorized military commanders to arrest and imprison any person reasonably suspected of treasonable practices, instructing such commanders to reply to any writ of *habeas corpus* to the effect that the imprisonment was by order of the President.

An attempt was made to prevent the enforcement of this proclamation, by an appeal to the Chief-Justice of the United States, Mr. Taney. A writ of *habeas corpus* was issued by him, while sitting in chambers at Baltimore, commanding the body of one Merryman to be brought before him. Merryman had been arrested and imprisoned by order of a military commander, under these directions of the President; and in obedience to these instructions he made return to the writ, refusing to deliver up his prisoner, stating the reason for his detention, and the authority of the President to suspend the writ of *habeas corpus.* Chief-Justice Taney filed an elaborate opinion, in which he maintained that the power to suspend the writ of *habeas corpus* was vested by the Constitution in Congress, and not in the Executive.[1] This opinion was ignored by the President, and arrests were made whenever the public safety was supposed to require it. This collision between the executive and judicial authority naturally caused a great deal of discussion, and numerous were the pamphlets, which were at the time issued to prove the true constitutional rule in the case. The most noteworthy of these arguments was that of Mr. Horace Binney, who took the side of the President, holding that he must of necessity possess the power to suspend the writ, since reason as well as experience proved that to be of value in the suppression of rebellions and insurrections, the right of suspension must be exercised promptly, more promptly at

---

[1] See *Ex parte* Merryman, Taney's Circuit-Court Decisions, Campbell's Rep., 246.

times than Congress can be expected to act. Public opinion remained divided on the question, and, finally, in order to remove all doubt from the legality of the suspension of the writ, Congress passed a law which authorized the President to suspend the writ by proclamation whenever the public exigencies required it.

The second case of supposed violation of constitutional limitations was in the establishment of military commissions to try, convict, and punish any one found guilty of treasonable practices. The power of these commissions was made to apply to those who were neither members of the military and naval forces of the United States nor prisoners of war. One Milligan was found, by one of these commissions, guilty of treason in attempting, in Indiana, to render aid to the Southern cause, and he was condemned to be hung. There was apparently no doubt of his guilt, and the sentence was approved by the President and Secretary of War. But the claim was made in his behalf, that since he was a civilian, and was living in a part of the country in which the ordinary courts, both State and Federal, were open for the administration of justice, the military commissions had no jurisdiction over his case; and that he was about to be deprived of his life, without due process of law, and in violation of the constitutional provision which guarantees the right of trial by jury.

The claim was made on the part of the United States that these constitutional provisions were only operative in time of peace, and that in time of war martial law must necessarily take the place of the ordinary law. That claim being conceded, it was held that the President, being intrusted with the prosecution of the war, must of necessity determine the time when, and the extent, both as to territory and the provisions of the law, to which the ordinary administration of the law must be superseded by the establishment of martial rule. That that was the constitutional rule of conduct during the war cannot be doubted. But after the cessation of hostilities, when the Milligan case was carried on appeal to the Supreme Court of the United States, it was held that the constitutional guaranties of trial by jury, etc., were in force during the war as well as in peace, and that the military commissions could not assume jurisdiction over offences which were not committed on the actual theatre of war, but in places away from the battle-fields, and where the ordinary courts were administering the law without obstruction. The chief-justice, and three associate justices concurred in the judgment of the majority of the court, but filed a separate opinion, in which the judgment was placed on the ground that Congress, and not the Executive, had the power, in the prosecution of the war, in order to suppress treasonable practices, to

establish military commissions over territory not included within the actual military operations, Mr.
Justice Davis expresses the conclusion of the court
thus :

" It follows from what has been said on this subject that there are
occasions when martial rule can be properly applied. If, in foreign
invasions or civil war, the courts are actually closed, and it is
impossible to administer criminal justice, according to the law, *then,*
on the theatre of active military operations, where war really prevails,
there is a necessity to furnish a substitute for the civil authority, thus
overthrown, to preserve the safety of the army and society ; and as no
power is left but the military, it is allowed to govern by martial rule
until the laws can have their free course. As necessity creates the
rule, so it limits its duration ; for, if this government is continued
after the courts are reinstated, it is a gross usurpation of power.
Martial rule can never exist where the courts are open and in the
proper and unobstructed exercise of their jurisdiction. It is also
confined to the locality of actual war. Because during the late
Rebellion it could not have been enforced in Virginia, where the
national authority was overturned and the courts driven out, it does not
follow that it should obtain in Indiana, where that authority was never
disputed and justice was always administered. And so in the case of a
foreign invasion, martial rule may become a necessity in one case,
when in another it would be mere lawless violence." [1]

I think the claim is readily substantiated that the
extraordinary powers exercised by the President of
the United States during the civil war are sanctioned
by the customs and usages of nations, and are employed in every war by the military commandants,
as necessity requires.[2] And it is very probable,
almost certain, that in any similar emergency the

---

[1] *Ex parte* Milligan, 4 Wall., 1, 127.
[2] See the arguments of counsel for Milligan and for the United
States, in *Ex parte* Milligan, 4 Wall., 1.

same powers will be claimed and exercised by the President, although they virtually make him a dictator, bound by no constitutional limitations which his discretion does not sanction, or the popular will does not impose. For, although the decision of the court in *ex parte* Milligan is a denial of these powers, and proclaims the President to be subject during the war to the same constitutional limitations which are strictly enforced in times of peace, it furnishes no constitutional rule for the emergencies of war, since the decision was rendered after the war had been brought to a close, and the pressure of military necessity had been removed. If the decision had been rendered during the war, when the Executive was actually exercising these extraordinary powers, and the Executive had submitted to the judgment of the court, a precedent would have then been established, from which the claim might have been deduced, that in all future wars the President, as commander-in-chief of the military forces, must, in dealing with dangerous persons, observe the same constitutional limitations which are enforced in times of peace. It is very likely that the decree of the court in the Milligan case would have met with the same treatment as did the decision of Chief-Justice Taney in the Merryman case, if it had been rendered during the prosecution of the war. But it is still more likely that the court would, under those circumstances, have yielded to the sense of military necessity, and have justified, instead of condemning, the employment of such powers.

The explanation of the apparent contradiction is not to be found in the maxim, *inter arma silent leges.* The laws are not silent in the presence of arms. In the substitution of martial rule for the civil authorities, there is only a change in the form of the administration of the law. The prevalent sense of right furnishes, in war as well as in peace, the norm for the formulation of rules of law. The military commander is not an arbitrary dictator and law-maker, although there is then no trial by jury, and no appeal to the ordinary courts of justice. Even though there be an inexplicable contradiction between the practices of military rule and the express limitations of the written Constitution, the rule which is actually enforced in time of war is the true constitutional rule, and not that which in time of peace the Supreme Court of the United States declares to be the proper rule. The history of the civil war teaches that the ordinary provisions of the written Constitution cannot be as rigidly enforced in times of great national emergencies as when the ordinary routine of governmental action meets with no serious obstruction. Whatever may be the proper deduction from the written Constitution, it is an established rule of the unwritten constitution that the President, in the exercise of his war powers, may substitute martial law for civil law as far as the public exigencies may in his judgment require. For the time being, the written limitations upon his power are completely laid aside, and he appears in the rôle of an almost absolute dictator.

But Mr. John Quincy Adams voices the opinion of many, when he claims that these extraordinary powers are necessary implications of the authority to declare and carry on war:

"In the authority given to Congress by the Constitution of the United States to declare war, all the powers, incident to war, are by necessary implication conferred upon the government of the United States. Now, the powers incidental to war are derived, not from any internal municipal source, but from the laws and usages of nations. There are, then, in the authority of Congress and the Executive, two classes of powers, altogether different in their nature, and often incompatible with each other—the war power and the peace power. The peace power is limited by regulations and restraints, by provisions prescribed within the Constitution itself. The war power is limited only by the law and usages of nations. The power is tremendous. *It is strictly constitutional, but it breaks down every barrier so anxiously erected for the protection of liberty, property, and life.*" [1]

---

[1] From a speech delivered in 1836, and quoted by Mr. B. F. Butler in his argument for the government in the case of *Ex parte Milligan*, 4 Wall., 104.

CHAPTER VIII.

CITIZENSHIP IN THE UNITED STATES.

THE claim has already been made[1] that, while most of the principles entering into the composition of the American Constitution are neither original nor novel,—the American constitutions being evolutionary forms of the British Constitution,—yet, there are a few principles which first found expression and full realization in our constitutional history. It was also claimed that the novel principles of our constitutional systems have not been fully realized and properly appreciated, until years of experience revealed their true character and effect.[2] One of these new principles was that of subjecting the same territory and the same people to the jurisdiction and control of two separate and autonomous governments, which, while they are bound together into one federal system of government, and divide the powers of government between them, are yet, in their own spheres, supreme and independent of each other, and

---

[1] See *ante* Chapter II., p. 37.   [2] See *ante* Chapter II., p. 33.

both have the power to directly command and compel the obedience of the individual citizen.

It is hardly necessary to assert that this is the chief fundamental principle of the American constitutional system, the adoption of which radically changed the character of the Union, from a league of States to a composite State of States, or, to borrow the language of Chief-Justice Chase[1]: "An indestructible Union composed of indestructible States." Before the adoption of the principle, there was no Federal State, only a league, whose very life depended upon the grace and favor of the States ; but, with its adoption, a Federal State was formed in such a mould, as it was thought and hoped, that it would not have the power to absorb, and destroy the autonomy of, the States. Therefore, with the adoption of the present Constitution of the United States, two separate governments came into being, the Federal and the State, each having its own separate sphere of action, and each in its sphere independent of the other. The Constitution does not explicitly make this declaration ; but it is a necessary consequence of the grant or reservation to each government of the power to act directly on the individual. The relations thus established between the individual and the two governments respectively, logically and necessarily make of the individual a citizen of each govern-

[1] Texas *v.* White, 7 Wall., 700, 725.

ment, so that a citizen of this country would be a citizen of the United States, as well as a citizen of the State in which he has his legal domicile.

The Constitution of the United States does not define or expressly recognize this dual citizenship, although both are inferentially recognized and referred to. It recognizes State citizenship in the clause,[1] which declares that " citizens of each State shall be entitled to all the privileges and immunities of citizens in the several States." Federal citizenship, however uncertain may be the view then entertained of its character, is nevertheless recognized in those clauses which provided, that no one is eligible to the position of President " excepting a natural-born citizen, or a citizen of the United States at the time of the adoption of the Constitution "[2]; of senator, unless he has been "nine years a citizen of the United States "[3]; or to the position of representative in Congress, unless he has been "seven years a citizen of the United States."[4] Like every other question which was raised before, and which divided, the constitutional convention, this was laid aside with a compromise, which constituted a partial and unsatisfactory recognition of the claims of both parties, the final settlement and adjustment of those claims being left to the future. It does not surprise

[1] Art. IV., sec. 2. [3] Art. I., sec. 3.
[2] Art. II., sec. 1. [4] Art. I., sec. 2.

one, therefore, to learn that a definite settlement of the limitations of this dual citizenship was not attained until there had been seventy-five or eighty years of contention, when the dream of the Websters [1] was first fully realized, by the judicial recognition of the dual citizenship, with all its attending consequences.

For forty years after the adoption of the Constitution, party strife over the fundamental questions of our constitutional system was not active, and hence a clear definition of citizenship was not then attained. Justice Story, in his commentaries on the Constitution, said, concerning citizenship : " It has always been well understood among jurists in this country, that the citizens of each State constitute the body-politic of each community, called the people of the States ; and that the citizens of each State in the Union are *ipso facto* citizens of the United States." It had also been held by Chief-Justice Marshall,[2] that a person, naturalized under the acts of Congress, became a citizen of the State in which he happened to reside.

But the question was not permitted to remain quietly in this unsettled condition, after the agitation in respect to slavery began. The State Rights' party were very plain in their claim of the limita-

---

[1] It will be remembered that the idea of a composite Federal State, with an independent autonomy for both Federal and State governments, originated with Pelatiah and Noah Webster. See *ante* Ch. II., p. 32.
[2] In Gassies *v.* Ballon, 6 Pet., 761.

tions of federal citizenship, holding that no one can be a citizen of the United States, except as a consequence of being the citizen of some State or Territory of the Union ; that citizenship of the State was the primary fact, while the citizenship of the United States was secondary and consequential.[1] The State Rights' doctrine of federal citizenship received judicial indorsement from the Supreme Court of the United States in the famous Dred Scott[2] case, in which it was held that while each State had the power to invest any one with State citizenship, not contemplated by the provisions of the Constitution, —for example, negroes, to whom citizenship was denied by the existing general constitutional rules, —yet such a person did not thereby acquire the equal participation in the rights and privileges of citizens in the several States, as was provided by the Constitution. Says Chief-Justice Taney :

---

[1] " If by citizen of the United States he [Senator Clayton, of Delaware] means a citizen at large, one whose citizenship extends to the entire geographical limits of the country without having a local citizenship in some State or Territory, a sort of citizen of the world, all I have to say is that such a citizen would be a perfect nondescript ; that not a single individual of this description can be found in the entire mass of our population. Notwithstanding all the pomp and display of eloquence on the occasion, every citizen is a citizen of some State or Territory, and as such, under an express provision of the Constitution, is entitled to all the privileges and immunities of citizens in the several States; and it is in this and no other sense that we are citizens of the United States."—Mr. Calhoun's argument on the " Force Bill." See his Works, II., 242.

[2] Scott *v.* Sanford, 19 How., 393.

"We must not confound the rights of citizenship which a State may confer within its own limits, and the rights of citizenship as a member of the Union. . . . He (such a person) may have all the rights and privileges of a citizen of a State, and yet not be entitled to the rights and privileges of a citizen in any other State. . . . Each State may . . . confer them (*i.e.*, the rights and privileges of State citizenship) upon an alien or any one it thinks proper, or upon any class or description of persons, yet he would not be a citizen in the sense in which that word is used in the Constitution of the United States, nor entitled to sue as such in one of its courts, nor to the privileges and immunities of a citizen in the other States. The rights which he would acquire would be restricted to the State which gave them. . . . No State, since the adoption of the Constitution, can, by naturalizing an alien, invest him with the rights and privileges secured to a citizen of a State under the Federal Government, although, so far as the State alone was concerned, he would undoubtedly be entitled to the rights of a citizen and clothed with all the rights and immunities which the Constitution and laws of the State attached to that character."

Mr. Justice Curtis dissented from the conclusion of the majority of the court, and held that

"it is left to each State to determine what free persons born within its limits shall be citizens of such State and thereby be citizens of the United States. . . . It must be remembered that, though the Constitution was to form a government, and under it the United States of America were to be one united sovereign nation to which loyalty and obedience on the one side, and from which protection and privileges on the other, would be due, yet the several sovereign States, whose people were then citizens, were not only to continue in existence, but with powers unimpaired, except so far as they were granted by the people to the national government. Among the powers unquestionably possessed by the several States was that of determining what persons should, and what persons should not, be citizens."

Judge Curtis was supposed to voice the sentiment of the opponents of the State Rights' party, and it is to be observed that, in this dissenting opinion, as well as in the opinion of the court, it was held that the citizenship of the United States was dependent upon, and proceeded from, citizenship of the State, the only point of difference being the power of the State to invest persons, who were not generally conceded the rights of citizens, with the citizenship of the United States by making them citizens of the State, the State Rights' party denying such a power to the State, and the opposition claiming for the State that right. The great hue and cry raised by the decision of the court, if it were not directed altogether against the *dicta* of the court, was certainly not caused by the subordination of national citizenship to State citizenship, but by the denial of national citizenship as a necessary consequence of State citizenship.

But a change was soon to be wrought in the views entertained on this constitutional question, by the arbitrament of the sword. When President Lincoln, by his proclamation, emancipated the slaves of the Southern States, he not only increased the relative strength of the National Government, but rendered necessary a radical change in the theories prevalent as to citizenship in the United States. If the National Government had the power to abolish slavery, in other words, to regulate the legal *status* of the individual, surely national citizenship must be paramount, while State citizenship is subordinate and

7

incidental, and this was the claim of Senator Lyman. Trumbull, and his supporters, in the presentation of the famous "Civil Rights Bill," in which it was declared that "all persons born in the United States. and not subject to any foreign power, excluding Indians not taxed, are citizens of the United States," and, as such, are entitled to the privileges and immunities of white citizens in the several States. But very many believed that the constitutional views on the subject, declared in the Dred Scott case, would be an obstacle to the procurement of a judicial recognition of the *post-bellum* doctrine, and hence the fourteenth amendment was proposed and adopted, in which it was declared that "all persons born or naturalized in the United States, and subject to the jurisdiction thereof, are citizens of the United States and of the State wherein they reside."

Not only does this amendment define national and State citizenship, and make the State citizenship a derivative of the national, but it proceeds to make a declaration concerning the rights and privileges of a citizen of the United States. It declares that "no State shall make or enforce any law which shall abridge the privileges and immunities of citizens of the United States ; nor shall any State deprive any person of life, liberty, or property without due process of law ; nor deny to any person within its jurisdiction the equal protection of the laws."

This constitutional declaration has been frequently brought before the court for construction ; but, before giving the view taken by the Supreme Court of the United States of its effect, I will attempt to show, by analogy from other congressional action, as well as by the language of the amendment, that the framers and enactors of it intended to place the negro, in his daily life, completely under the control of the National Government. *First*, as to the language of the amendment. Not content with denying to the States the authority to abridge by legislation "the privileges and immunities of citizens of the United States,"—which, by the way, was a useless prohibition, if by the privileges and immunities were not meant those fundamental privileges and immunities which inhere in the definition of citizenship,—the amendment proceeds to declare in effect what those privileges and immunities are, viz. : "Nor shall any State deprive any person of life, liberty, or property without due process of law ; nor deny to any person within its jurisdiction the equal protection of the laws." A literal interpretation of this amendment would give to the United States Supreme Court the power at any time to inquire into the effect of State legislation on the fundamental privileges and immunities of the citizen, which, before the adoption of the amendment, were exclusively within the control and protection of the State governments. That that was the intention of the political leaders is easily shown by the speeches in Congress. Senator Trumbull, in the debate on the Civil Rights bill, said:

" But, sir, what rights do citizens of the United States have ? To be a citizen of the United States carries with it some rights; and what are they ? They are those inherent fundamental rights which belong to free citizens or freemen in all countries, such as the rights enumerated in this bill [to make and enforce contracts, to sue, be parties and give evidence, to inherit, purchase, lease, sell, hold, and convey real estate and personal property, and to full and equal benefit of all laws and proceedings for the security of person and property, as enjoyed by white citizens] ; and they belong to them in all the States in the Union. The right of American citizenship means something."

And in another place :

" What are they [*i.e.*, the rights of a citizen of the United States]? The right of personal security, the right of personal liberty, and the right to acquire and enjoy property." [1]

We would likewise be forced to take this view of the operation of this amendment by the conviction that any other construction would make this part of the amendment " a vain and idle enactment." [2]

---

[1] *Congressional Globe*, 1st Sess., 39th Cong., p. 1757.

[2] " It [the Fourteenth Amendment] assumes that there are . . . privileges and immunities which belong of right to citizens, as such, and ordains that they shall not be abridged by State legislation. If this inhibition has no reference to privileges and immunities of this character, but only refers, as held by the majority of the court in their opinion, to such privileges and immunities as were before its adoption specially designated in the Constitution or necessarily implied as belonging to citizens of the United States, it was a vain and idle enactment which accomplished nothing, and most unnecessarily excited Congress and the people on its passage. With privileges and immunities thus designated or implied, no State could ever have

Flushed with a decisive victory over the State
Rights' party, obtained in the highest court of
appeals known to politics, and inflamed by the
enactment of the so-called Black laws by several of
the Southern legislatures, which were intended to
repress and oppress the negro in every sphere of
life; without thought of the far-reaching effect of
their proposed legislation, the Republican party proceeded to make laws, which would be strong enough
to protect the negro in his freedom.   If the consti-

---

interfered by its laws, and no constitutional provision was required to
inhibit such interference. . . . But if the amendment refers to
the natural and inalienable rights which belong to all citizens, the
inhibition has a profound significance and consequence."—Mr. Justice Field's dissenting opinion in Slaughter-house cases.

  "The privileges and immunities of a citizen of the United States
include, among other things, the fundamental rights of life, liberty,
and property, and also the rights which pertain to him by reason of
his membership of a nation . . . without authority (to secure
such rights and privileges) any government claiming to be national is
glaringly defective.   The construction adopted by the majority of my
brethren is, in my judgment, much too narrow.   It defeats by a
limitation not anticipated the intent of those by whom the instrument
was framed, and of those by whom it was adopted.   To the extent of
that limitation it turns, as it were, what was meant for bread, into
stone."—Justice Swayne's dissenting opinion in Slaughter-house cases.

  "I think sufficient has been said to show that citizenship is not an
empty name, but that, in this country, at least, it has connected with
it certain rights, privileges, and immunities of the greatest importance, and to say that these rights and immunities attach only to State
citizenship, and not to citizenship of the United States, appears to me
to evince a very narrow and insufficient estimate of constitutional history and the rights of men, not to say the rights of the American
people."—Mr. Justice Bradley's dissenting opinion in Slaughter-house
cases.

tutional amendment had been allowed to have its full literal effect, the end obtained would be what Madison, Randolph, and Hamilton proposed, in the constitutional convention of 1787, to accomplish by the Virginia plan of government, viz.: the establishment of a strong national government and the subjection of the States to the condition of provinces, and this government would have very soon ceased to be a federal government, save in name. I do not suppose that the majority of those, whose votes brought about the adoption of this amendment, intended it to have this effect in general; but it is very certain that they desired and intended to deprive the Southern people of all legal opportunity to keep the negro in political and social subjection, and, thus, to frustrate the realization of what they considered the legitimate results of the war. But this special end could not be attained without putting an end, everywhere, to local self-government in the American sense.

That disastrous result was, however, happily averted by the bold and courageous stand taken by the Supreme Court of the United States, when this amendment was brought before them for construction. Feeling assured that the people in their cooler moments would not have sanctioned the far-reaching effects of their action; that they lost sight of the general effect in their eager pursuit of a special end, the court dared to withstand the popular will as expressed in the letter of this amendment ; and, by giving it a narrow and close construction, to cut off its injurious consequences, although in doing so, as was stated by Justice Swayne, " it turns what was meant for bread, into stone," and in very large measure prevented the realization of the end expressly had in view, viz.: the transfer of all the rights of the negro, as a citizen, to the protection of the United States Government.

The opinion of the court in the Slaughter-house cases[1] was delivered by Mr. Justice Miller, and concurred in by a majority of the court, but dissented from by four justices of the court, of whom three justices, Field, Swayne, and Bradley, wrote dissenting opinions.

· The argument of the court was that this amendment, when considered in the light of history, recognized two separate citizenships, the citizenship of the United States and the citizenship of the States, and each citizenship had its corresponding and different privileges and immunities. The privileges and immunities of the citizens of the States were defined to be " those privileges and immunities which are fundamental, which belong of right to the citizens of all free governments, and which have at all times been enjoyed by citizens of the several States which

[1] 16 Wall., 37, 57.

compose this Union, from the time of their becoming free, independent, and sovereign. What these fundamental principles are it would be more tedious than difficult to enumerate.[1] They may all, however, be comprehended under the following general heads: protection by the government, with the right to acquire and possess property of every kind, and to pursue and obtain happiness and safety, subject, nevertheless, to such restraints as the government may prescribe for the general good of the whole."[2]

After stating that "it would be the vainest show of learning," to show that up to the adoption of the *post-bellum* amendments these privileges were not under the protection of the United States government, the court say ·

" Was it the purpose of the fourteenth amendment, by the simple declaration that no State should make or enforce any law which shall abridge the privileges and immunities of *citizens of the United States,* to transfer the security and protection of all the civil rights which we have mentioned, from the States to the Federal Government ? And where it is declared that Congress shall have the power to enforce that article, was it intended to bring within the power of Congress the entire domain of civil rights, heretofore belonging exclusively to the States ?

" All this and more must follow, if the proposition of the plaintiffs in error be sound. For not only are these rights subject to the

---

[1] See Tiedeman's " Limitations of Police Power," for a detailed discussion and application of them to the daily experiences of the individual.

[2] Washington, J., in Corfield *v.* Coryell, 4 Wash. C. C., 371 ; and adopted by the Supreme Court of the United States, in Ward *v.* State of Maryland, 12 Wall., 430.

control of Congress, whenever in its discretion any of them are supposed to be abridged by State legislation, but that body may also pass
laws in advance, limiting and restricting the exercise of legislative
power by the States, in their most ordinary and usual functions, as, in
its judgment, it may think proper on all such subjects. And still
further, such a construction, followed by the reversal of the judgment
of the Supreme Court of Louisiana in these cases, would constitute
this court a perpetual censor upon all legislation of the States on the
civil rights of their own citizens, with authority to nullify such as it
did not approve as consistent with those rights as they existed at the
time of the adoption of the amendment. The argument we admit is
not always the most conclusive which is drawn from the consequences
urged against the adoption of a particular construction of an instrument. But when, as in the case before us, these consequences are so
serious, so far-reaching and pervading, so great a departure from the
structure and spirit of our institutions, when the effect is to fetter and
degrade the State governments by subjecting them to the control of
Congress, in the exercise of powers heretofore universally conceded to
them of the most ordinary and fundamental character ; when in fact ·
it radically changes the whole theory of the relations of the State and
Federal governments to each other, and of both these governments to
the people,—the argument has a force that is irresistible, in the absence
of language which expresses such a purpose too clearly to admit
of doubt." [1]

The court then proceed to eumerate what are to
be considered as the privileges and immunities of the
United States which the States cannot abridge, and
which are as follows :

" To come to the seat of government to assert any claim upon that
government, to transact any business with it, to seek its protection, to
share its offices, to engage in administering its functions.

" Free access to its seaports, through which all operations of foreign
commerce are conducted ; to the sub-treasuries, land-offices, and courts
of justice in the several States.

" To demand the care and protection of the Federal Government
over life, liberty, and property, when on the high seas or within the
jurisdiction of a foreign government.

---

[1] Pp. 77, 78.

" To peaceably assemble and petition for redress of grievances.

" The writ of *habeas corpus.*

" To use the navigable waters of the United States, however they may penetrate the territory of the several States.

" To become a citizen of any one of the several States by a *bona-fide* residence therein."

The judgment of the court was that these were the only privileges and immunities whose protection is provided for in this amendment, and that the ordinary and relatively more important privileges and immunities of citizenship " are not privileges and immunities of citizens of the United States within the meaning of the clause of the fourteenth amendment under consideration."

The noble fundamental purpose of the court in checking the literal operation of the fourteenth amendment is to be found expressed in the closing paragraphs of the opinion.

" But however pervading this sentiment [the desire for a strong national government] and however it may have contributed to the adoption of the amendments we have been considering, we do not see in those amendments any purpose to destroy the main features of the general system. Under the pressure of all the excited feeling growing out of the war, our statesmen have still believed that the existence of the States, with powers for domestic and local government, including the regulation of civil rights—the rights of person and of property—was essential to the complex form of government, though they have thought proper to impose additional limitations on the States, and to confer additional power on that of the nation.

" But whatever fluctuations may be seen in the history of public opinion on this subject during the period of our national existence, we think it will be found that this court, so far as its functions required, has always held with a steady and an even hand the balance between State and Federal power, and we trust that such may continue to be the history of its relation to that subject so long as it shall have duties to perform which demand of it a construction of the Constitution or of any of its parts."

This instance furnishes one of the most striking proofs of the thesis, that political constitutions are a growth, evolved from all the forces of society, both material and spiritual.

We find first a novel principle of politics, *i.e.*, that of a dual government, with separate autonomies, proposed and adopted by a nation, but its consequences yet unknown. There is a faint recognition at once even in the written Constitution of one consequence, viz., a dual citizenship, but the relative strength and obligation of the two separate citizenships are not referred to. After remaining in doubt for many years, it is claimed by the State Rights' party—and the claim is indorsed and pronounced to be the supreme law of the land by the Supreme Court of the United States—that the citizenship of the United States is an incident of, and depends for existence upon, the citizenship of the States. This decision of the Supreme Court was practically overruled by the findings of the court of war, but in order to provide a technical repeal, an amendment to the Federal Constitution was adopted, declaring the federal citizenship to be the primary and all-important thing, while the citizenship of the States was subordinate and incidental to it. While it is very likely that the people did not wish to do more, except possibly in the South, than to establish the perpetual supremacy of the National Government and of national citizenship over State governments and State citizenship, the literal scope was such, that a strict enforcement of the amendment would have resulted in a complete reduction of the States to the condition of provinces, and a grant to the United States Government of a supervisory control over the smallest concerns of life.

Alarmed at the peril in which the people stood, and deeply impressed with the necessity of providing a remedy, the Supreme Court of the United States averted the evil consequences by keeping the operation of the amendment within the limits which they felt assured would have been imposed by the people, if their judgment had not been blinded with passion, and which in their cooler moments they would ratify. The so-called strict-constructionists may assert that this was an unwarranted exercise of the judicial power, and one that could become the effective instrument of tyranny; this may be so. But if by constitutional law we mean those rules which serve to define and limit the powers of government, we must pronounce the decision of the court in the Slaughter-house cases to be a successful modification of the rule found in the fourteenth amendment. That this reflected the prevalent, but perhaps then unexpressed, sense of right, is proven by the fact that no attempt was made to overrule it by additional legislation; nor was there any outcry against it, after the people had recovered from their surprise at this bold limitation of their written commands. Although there have been some material but minor modifications of the rule in subsequent decisions, the ruling of the court in these cases is still a part of the constitutional law of the United States, serving as a bulwark to the States in their struggle for autonomy and self-government.

CHAPTER IX.

STATE SOVEREIGNTY AND RIGHT OF SECESSION.

FROM the adoption of the Kentucky resolutions of 1798, until the hard logic of war placed the stamp of illegality upon the doctrine, there had always been a strong and influential party, whose fundamental tenets were that the Union was a confederation of sovereign States, which are bound by the laws and the Constitution of the United States, as long as they remain in the Union ; but which may, separately and at their own discretion, withdraw or secede from the Union, whenever they consider the confederation detrimental to themselves. Each State, as a sovereign, was conceded this power. There were, of course, parties which asserted the sovereignty of the United States, and denied to the States this right of secession.

This contest of principle was another consequence of the failure of the constitutional convention to settle definitely the true relation of the States to each other and to the Federal State. I do not believe that the arguments for and against the right

of secession, which are to be found in the speeches
of Webster and Calhoun, and of Clay and Hayne,
and in histories and other books without number,
present the matter in its true light. It is not incon-
sistent with the highest respect for the great men,
who participated with so much effect and power in
these political debates of the Senate, for the claim to
be made that there was a failure on both sides to
appreciate and bring to light the real scientific facts
of the situation, which justify logically the ultimate
settlement of the question. It is with some hesitation that I proceed to present what I consider the
true view; but if there is no defect in my major
premise, as explained and developed in the first and
second chapters, the conclusion, to which I come in
the discussion of the doctrine of State sovereignty
and the right of secession, is irresistible.

In this contest, the South was the aggressive
party, while the North only resisted the extreme
conclusion of the South in respect to the right of a
single State to secede, whenever it was to its interest
to do so. The Southern claim was that this Union
was a confederation of independent, sovereign States;
that the Federal Government was the creature of the
States, having only that power which the States delegated to it, and that it may be shorn of its power
over any single State, whenever that State, in consequence of the violation of the constitutional limita-

tions by the United States Government, of which the State is to be the final judge,—decides to secede from the Union, and establish itself as an independent nation.

Without undertaking to present any lengthy statement of the arguments *pro* and *con*, it may be pithily stated that the Southern claim of secession rested upon two fundamental principles. One was that of the Declaration of Independence, that " all governments derive their just powers from the consent of the governed "; the general conclusion being that the governed may *legally* withdraw that consent, whenever the powers have been tyrannically employed for the oppression of the people. The second principle was that sovereignty was reposed under our constitutional system in the States; and that, in consequence of this fundamental fact, the Union was, under this Constitution as under the Articles of Confederation, only a league or confederation of sovereign States, which combined for purposes of mutual protection, and which *consented* to a grant to their general agent or government of those powers which were necessary to the promotion of their general welfare; but that any one of these sovereign States, under an application of the first principle (*i.e.*, government by consent of the governed), may withdraw from the Union, whenever it considers itself wronged by the General Government or its interests prejudiced by remaining in the Union. The opponents of the Southern theory have uniformly admitted the correctness of the principle, that the just powers of government are derived from the consent of the governed ; but claim that this Constitution changed the Union from a league into a nation, and vested the sovereignty in the people of the United States.

Both principles are so far false as to be misleading, and the general prevalence of these misconceptions has, in my judgment, been the chief cause of the greatest civil war history has ever recorded. I do not wish to be understood as losing sight of the demand for the abolition of slavery as a cause of the war. On the contrary, I recognize it as the immediate occasion of the war ; but I claim that the war might have been averted if the entire Southern people had not been educated in the political faith which rested upon these two misleading principles.

The natural and uncontrollable impulse of the human mind is to demand a satisfactory basis for the exercise of governmental authority. The fundamental query of political philosophy is, By what right do those in authority command your and my obedience ? This query has at all times required an answer, but it has never been so difficult to give a satisfying answer as now. In the days when the belief in the divine right of kings was general, and

8

perhaps universal, a satisfactory answer to the question was readily obtained. No one questioned the
right of the Creator of all things to command our
obedience ; and if the kings were the vicegerents of
God upon earth, their authority was derived from
God. But when faith in the divine right of kings
weakened, and was finally repudiated by the leaders,
and perhaps also by the mass, of the civilized people
of the world as a fundamental basis for governmental authority, the philosophical minds of the world,
under the lead of the English Hobbes and the
French Rousseau, developed as a substitute the doctrine of a social contract. If governmental power
was not derived from God, it must be derived from
the people, who by common agreement established
the societies in which we live. This social contract
involved, when the people entered into the social
organization, the surrender of rights which were
enjoyed by individuals in a state of nature, so far
as such a surrender may be necessary to the common
weal. None of these dreamers actually believed
that while the people, in prehistoric times, were
living without social organization of any kind, they
suddenly came to the conclusion that it was good
for them to organize into political bodies and to subject themselves to certain rules for the common
good. They did not believe any such marvellous
tale. Starting out with the declaration of the mutual

equality of all men, they could not justify in reason
the acquisition by the few of a control of the many,
except upon the hypothesis that this subjection of
the mass to the few was voluntary. But that
hypothesis is not consistent with any other theory
than that all governments are founded upon a social
contract. They knew that the contract was a fiction,
but they had become so accustomed, as we still are,
to the use of fictions in the administration of the
law, that they were not conscious of the violence
done to the facts of the case. The only way of
solving the metaphysical difficulty that confronted
them was in the use of this fiction, and if the facts
did not fit and support the hypothesis, they were in
a frame of mind to pronounce it all the worse for the
facts.[1] This doctrine was in the air everywhere when
the Government and Constitution of the United
States were established, and although political scien-
tists have generally repudiated it, it still has a hold
upon the popular mind, and dominates the legal
thought of this country.[2]

---

[1] "All men have one common original : they participate in one
common nature, and have one common right. No reason can be
advanced why one man should exercise any power or pre-eminence
over his fellow-creatures more than another, unless they have voluntarily vested him with it. Since, then, Americans have not, by any
act of theirs, empowered the British Parliament to make laws for
them, it follows they can have no just authority to do it."—"Hamilton's Works," I., 6 (Lodge's edition).

[2] Not many months ago (1890) the Senate of the United States
adopted a resolution congratulating the people of Brazil on the estab-

The form which the theory generally assumes in the United States is that " governments are insti- tuted among men, deriving their just powers from the consent of the governed " (Declaration of Inde- pendence).

While that doctrine is true in the sense that all governments rest upon the acquiescence in their decrees of the great mass of the people whom they rule, it is not true that the power is derived from the consent of all the governed. Confessedly, the power to control the actions of women and children is not derived from their consent, not even in the land of so-called universal suffrage. And where the suffrage of male adults is limited to those who possess an educational and property qualification, the fallacy of the doctrine becomes still more manifest. It is absurd to say that the thieves and thugs who infest society ever subscribed their consent to the criminal laws of the land. They have not even acquiesced in their establishment, except so far as an over- powering force has compelled them to yield partial obedience.

But it may be urged that by this doctrine is meant not that the consent of each and every individual to

lishment by them of a government depending for its powers upon the consent of the governed ; and the decisions of the courts and the practical treatises on constitutional law still teem with references to the natural rights of man, and a surrender of a part of them upon entry into organized society.—See *ante* Ch. VI.

the laws of the country must be obtained before
they can be rightfully enforced, but that the government derives its just powers from the consent of the
majority of the people whom it rules. But, granting
that this is a proper limitation upon the meaning of
the postulate, and forbearing to do more than make
the claim that the limitation is a fatal admission of
the insufficiency of the theory, since it would not
then furnish any justification for the control of the
minority by the majority, even then the theory will
not fit in with the facts. It is to be supposed that
no one would question the truth of the proposition
that only those rule who have the right to exercise
the electoral franchise. If one cannot vote in the
elections of the country, he cannot be said to have
given his consent to the enactment and enforcement
of the laws.

Now the population of the United States was in
1880 fifty millions, and it would not be too liberal
an estimate to put the population in 1888 at sixty
millions. I believe the census of 1890 will show a
still greater increase. It will without doubt be conceded that the presidential canvass of 1888 was a
very warm contest, and brought out the full strength
of both parties; and that almost every one voted in
that election who had a right to vote. The total
number of votes cast at that election for all the presidential candidates was 11,388,038. The eleven mil-

lions, therefore, determined among themselves who shall exercise governmental authority over the sixty millions. On what theory of consent can it be explained that the eleven millions had a right to command the obedience of the forty-nine millions? The authority of the eleven millions and of their governmental representatives, to control the actions of the silent, non-participating forty-nine millions, rests upon no other legal basis than that which supports the right of the law-makers to compel the thieves and thugs of society to render obedience to their edicts. It is because the eleven millions have the power to compel the obedience of any one of the forty-nine millions, that he renders obedience to the laws of the country. The moral influence of the eleven millions over the mass of the forty-nine millions, rather than the possession of the superior physical force, is what secures the subjection of the many to the commands of the few. But still the proposition remains true, that the exercise of political power by the few does not rest upon the consent of the subject and silent majority, but upon the possession by the few of the superior strength, both moral and material. And the commands of these few constitute the law, whatever may be their inherent viciousness or inequity. Moral reasons may be assigned for pronouncing a particular exercise of authority by the ruling power to be unrighteous or unjust; but no exercise of authority by the ruling power in the land can ever be called illegal.

Not only is it true as a fact, that governments do not derive their just powers from the consent of the governed, but it is not even believed in by the people, except as a part of their philosophy. It is not a part of their practical politics, as the following clipping from a current number of a leading journal will show:

"We shall never go back to the crude attempt of the Puritans to secure the purity of the ballot by confining the suffrage to church members ; but we may well question whether we have not gone quite too far in the opposite direction, in giving the suffrage to everybody regardless of either moral or intellectual qualifications, and whether it is not high time we took some measures to make conscience more powerful at the polling-booth." [1]

Who is meant by "we" in this extract? Until our attention is directly called to it, it does not appear strange to us that the distinguished editor should refer to some aggregation of the people, as having in them the totality of governmental power, by the personal pronoun "we," without any other description. And it is very likely that the great majority of the readers of this editorial, if they had been questioned, would have stated that the writer was referring to the power of the people to regulate their concerns for the general welfare. But that could not have been the thought of the writer; nor did the

---

[1] *Christian Union*, editorial, "Political Puritanism," Jan. 1, 1890.

readers, whether they indorsed or disapproved the proposition, base their conclusion upon the fundamental principle that the people *en masse* were referred to under the personal pronoun "we." For it is manifestly absurd to urge that the mass of the people, in whom it is claimed is reposed all political power, should confine the exercise of suffrage to the few. Whether consciously or unconsciously, the writer must have had in mind the antagonism of good and evil in politics, and under the personal pronoun "we" he was referring to those individual units of the political world, which constituted the good elements, and which had the power to control the evil elements. And it does not need to go to any length to show that the good elements in the body politic are not always in a numerical majority, even when they effectively control the actions of the vicious and evil. We have in this casual instance,— taken from a journal noted for its carefully prepared and well-digested editorials and news-matter,—a striking proof of the practical want of faith in the people in the doctrine of universal or popular suffrage. They do not really believe that political power resides in the mass of the people. When we lay aside our political dreaming, and come down to a consideration of the plain facts of political science, we are forced to the conclusion that there is no community in the world whose inhabitants stand on an absolute equality before the law, and hence no community in whose entire population the supreme power may be said to be vested. All governments are either monarchies or oligarchies.[1]

The fallacy of the doctrine that the government "derives its just powers from the consent of the governed," is still further exposed when it is remembered that most of the laws now in force were enacted before the present generations were born. They acquiesce in their enforcement, or rather the laws are enforced against the rebellious, because the present generations in the mass have acquired the habit of voluntarily obeying them, and desire their enforcement against others, in order to prevent injury to themselves. And it is also true that the laws will cease to be enforced as soon as public opinion, under the operation of the social forces, undergoes a change, and those who form public opinion generally justify the doing of the things forbidden by the pre-existing rules of law. But it cannot be said that the enactment of any law rests for

---

[1] "Nor, again, can sovereignty be said to reside in the entire community—an error to which French writers on public law seem especially liable. Their meaning may perhaps be that no body of individuals except the entirety of the people ought to be recognized as superior ; but a dogma like this is something very different from the statement of a fact ; and the truth is that no government corresponding with the description exists in the world. All politics are either monarchies or oligarchies, since even in the most popular women and minors are excluded from political functions."—Sir Henry Maine, in "Papers," etc. (1855), vol. i., pt. i., p. 30.

its authority upon the consent of the governed. The living part of municipal law—having no reference to the dead letters—consists of those rules of human conduct which the great mass of people habitually and spontaneously obey, and which they compel the rebellious minority to obey, in order to prevent injury to the law-abiding individual or to the commonwealth. If that be the true definition of the law, then all governmental authority rests upon the commands, not of a dead generation, but of a living generation. And even the treaties and other compacts which a past generation makes,—leaving the ethical element out of consideration,—are legally binding upon the present generation only so far as they acquiesce in their observance, or are required by a superior force to observe them.

The binding authority of law, therefore, does not rest upon any edict of the people in the past; it rests upon the present will of those who possess the political power.

The other political fallacy is wrapped up in the notion of sovereignty. Political writers of all shades of opinion speak of the sovereignty of the state, the sovereignty of the king, the sovereignty of the people; and our own history is filled with the discussions concerning the location of sovereignty in a federal state. The advocates of the State Rights' theory maintain that, since the Federal Government was the creation of the States, sovereignty must reside in the States as separate bodies-politic, while the National parties claim that sovereignty resides in the people of the United States as one body-politic. Notwithstanding the looseness which characterizes the use of the term " sovereignty " in these discussions, the elements of personality and of omnipotence are always present, more or less, in the meaning attached to the term, showing a close adherence to its original meaning, when there was one individual who claimed to be the omnipotent ruler of the people by divine right. Hence the claim is made that sovereignty is indivisible and subject to no legal limitation. As long as this definition of sovereignty is applied to an absolute monarchy—for example, like the Empire of Russia—no serious difficulties are experienced in making use of the notion of sovereignty in the practical explanations of the phenomena of political life. But when the notion is applied to a popular government, a government which, whatever its form, is founded upon a recognition of the repose of the ultimate political power in some part of the people, the most painful sort of confusion results. I will not attempt to give in this connection a summary of the views entertained by the political writers of Europe and America concerning the location and character of the sovereignty in a country ruled by a popular government. Such explanations are to be found in many books and need not be repeated. For it seems to me that if the reader has up to this point conceded the correctness of my propositions concerning the origin and development of law, both public and private, he will have no need for these political abstractions. To him sovereignty has no practical meaning which does not make it synonymous with supreme power; and the sovereign or sovereigns are the individual or individuals who together constitute the repository of the supreme power of the land; not the aggregation of individuals which have been declared by a past generation to be the repository of the supreme power of the land, but that aggregation of individuals which do now possess the supreme power of the land. Hence the written Constitution cannot locate the sovereignty of this country. It may be claimed, without the fear of successful contradiction, that prior to the present Constitution sovereignty resided in the States; because we know that the Federal Government had not the power to compel the obedience of the States, and was under the Articles of Confederation denied all control over the individual citizens. And it may also be claimed that the present written Constitution contains nothing which might serve as a transfer of sovereignty from the States to the people of the United States. But that Constitution did make a transfer possible by giving to the Federal Government direct control of the individual. Then began a contest for the supremacy between these two forces, the forces of disintegration and the forces of centralization. According to the definition of sovereignty here given, its location remained doubtful and could not be settled until the result of the civil war demonstrated the superiority of the forces of centralization.

It would seem plain, therefore, that the right of secession cannot be proved or disproved by reference to the written words of the Constitution, or to the opinions and intentions of those who helped to frame the Constitution and found the government. For, since all law derives its binding authority from the present commands of those who now control and mould public opinion, and not from any original compact or consent of the governed, the supreme power is in that aggregation of individuals, which now has the ability to enforce obedience to its commands. The people of the United States exercised supreme power over the State of South Carolina and prohibited its secession from the Union for the same . reason and on the same ground as they exercised supreme power over the Mexicans, who became American citizens, in consequence of a cession by Mexico to the United States of the territory in which they lived. It was because in both cases the United States had the ability to assert supreme power over the objecting individuals. The fact that the United

States hold these peoples in subjection makes the people of the United States the depositary of sovereign power; and whenever that fact ceases to exist, and the supreme power has in fact been transferred to some other aggregation of individuals, sovereignty will no longer be in the people of the United States.

But if that be the case, one might ask what becomes of that clause of the Declaration of Independence, in which it is claimed "that, whenever any form of government becomes destructive of these ends (*i.e.*, the guaranty of the inalienable rights of man), it is the right of the people to alter or abolish it, and to institute a new government, laying its foundation on such principles, and organizing its powers in such form, as to them shall seem most likely to effect their safety and happiness"? What is the meaning of this declaration, if it be true that that aggregation of individuals is sovereign, which has the actual ability to enforce obedience?

The difficulty is occasioned only by a confusion of abstract moral and actual legal claims. A claim is abstractly moral or immoral, rightful or wrongful, according to its inherent character and its good or bad effect upon the general welfare, independent of the ability to assert and compel its recognition; but it is legal or illegal, right or wrong legally, as it accords with, or opposes, the commands of those who possess the political power of the country. It is evident, therefore, that the exercise of the right, claimed in the American Declaration of Independence, to alter or abolish any government which fails to secure to the individual protection to life, liberty, and the pursuit of happiness, however justifiable in morals it might be at times, is never legal, always illegal; for the aim of those who exercise this right is to overthrow those who are the existing sovereigns, and whose commands are the law. Revolutions are nothing more than successful rebellions, while rebellions differ from revolutions only in the fact that the former are unsuccessful. Both have their beginning in unlawful acts, even though the cause be righteous. But just as soon as the rebellion becomes a revolution, the former sovereign power is overthrown, and another power, represented by the revolutionists, takes its place. With this shifting of the supreme power, a radical change is effected in the character of the actions of the opposing parties. The acts of the revolutionists then become legal, while the acts of the supporters of the old government become illegal.

We are now prepared to state the conclusion of the argument. If the powers of government are derived from the ability of those who command to enforce obedience, and the sovereignty of a nation resides in those who for the time being possess the political power, the right of secession is nothing more than

the right of revolution, morally justifiable or unjus-
tifiable, according to the character of the causes
which induced its exercise, but never legal, until its
successful exercise has wrought a transfer of the
political power from one aggregation of individuals
to another.

CHAPTER X.

FREQUENTLY, during the first century of our national existence, the government of the United States has assumed powers, which were highly essential to the promotion of the general welfare, but which were not expressly delegated to the Federal Government. The exercise of such powers has always met with the vehement objection of the party in opposition—although each of the great national parties has in turn exercised such questionable powers, whenever public necessities or party interests seemed to require it—the objection being that the Constitution did not authorize the exercise of the power, since there was no delegation of it by the Constitution. Popular opinion, concerning the fundamental character of the Federal Government, which had been lately established, was formulated in the adoption of the tenth amendment to the Constitution, which provides that " the powers, not delegated to the United States by the Constitution, nor prohibited by it to the States, are reserved to the States, respectively or to the people." Relying upon this amendment as the authority for it, it has become the generally recognized rule of constitutional construction, that, adopting the language of an eminent writer on constitutional law, " the government of the United States is one of enumerated powers, the National Constitution being the instrument which specifies, and in which the authority should be found for the exercise of, any power which the national government assumes to possess. In this respect it differs from the constitutions of the several States, which are not grants of powers to the States, but which apportion and impose restrictions upon the powers which the States inherently possess." [1]

The so-called " strict constructionists " have maintained that the United States can exercise no power but what is *expressly* granted by the Constitution. But this rule was at times applied so rigidly by the party in opposition, whenever it was proposed to prevent the enactment of a law which was obnoxious to them, that the right was denied to the United States Government to exercise even those rights

---

[1] Cooley, Const. Lim., 10, 11. See, also, to the same effect, Marshall, Ch.-J., in Gibbons *v.* Ogden, 9 Wheat., 1 ; Story, J., in Martin *v.* Hunter's Lessee, 1 Wheat., 304, 326 ; Waite, Ch.-J., in United States *v.* Cruikshanks, 92 U. S., 542 ; Calder *v.* Bull, 3 Dall., 386; Trade Mark Cases, 100 U. S., 82 ; Briscoe *v.* Bank of Kentucky, 11 Pet., 257 ; Gilman *v.* Philadelphia, 3 Wall., 713 ; and numerous judicial utterances of the same import in the State reports.

which, although not expressly delegated, were so necessary to the effectuation of the express powers, that it cannot be supposed that the framers of the Constitution did not intend to grant them. In numerous instances this question of constitutional construction has been brought for settlement before the Supreme Court of the United States; and it is now firmly settled that the Federal Government can exercise, not only the powers which are expressly granted, but also those powers, the grant of which can be fairly implied from the necessity of assuming them, in order to give effect to the express grant of powers. "The government of the United States can claim no powers which are not granted to it by the Constitution ; and the powers actually granted must be such as are expressly granted, or given by necessary implication."[1]

Although the United States Supreme Court has never, in its numerous decisions on constitutional construction, departed from the doctrine that the United States Government may exercise powers which are implied from the express grant of powers, it is worthy of note that for nineteen years one justice—Mr. Justice Daniel of Virginia—consistently dissented from every judgment of the court which was based upon the recognition of any implied

[1] Story, J., in Martin *v.* Hunter's Lessee, 1 Wheat., 304, 326 ; Marshall, Ch.-J., in Gibbons *v.* Ogden, 9 Wheat., 1, 187, etc. See preceding note.

power. His persistent claim was that "the Constitution itself is nothing more than an enumeration of general abstract rules, promulged by the several States for the guidance or control of their creature or agent, the federal government, which for their exclusive benefit they were about to call into being. Apart from these abstract rules, the Federal Government can have no functions and no existence."[1]

This doctrine of implied powers gave to the Federal Constitution that elasticity of application without which the permanency of the Federal Government would have been seriously endangered.[2] But at the same time it produced the very effect, in a greater or less degree, the fear of which urged the strict constructionists to oppose its adoption, viz.: that it would open the way to the most strained construction of express grants of power, in order to justify the exercise of powers that could not be fairly implied from the express grants. Indeed, the country

---

[1] Opinion of Justice Daniel in Marshall *v.* B. & O. R. R. Co., 16 How., 346.

[2] " While the principles of the Constitution should be preserved with a most guarded caution, it is at once the dictate of wisdom and enlightened patriotism to avoid that narrowness of interpretation which would dry up all its vital powers, or compel the government—as was done under the Confederation—to break down all constitutional barriers, and trust for its vindication to the people, upon the dangerous political maxim that the safety of the people is the supreme law (*salus populi suprema lex*), a maxim which might be used to justify the appointment of a dictator, or any other usurpation."—Story on Constitution, § 1,292. See Chapter VII. on The Suspension of the Writ of Habeas Corpus during the Civil War.

has often been presented with the spectacle of
United States, as well as State, judges and legislators engaged in justifying questionable but necessary
assumptions of power by the general government, by
laboriously twisting, turning, and straining the plain
literal meaning of the constitutional provisions, seek-
ing to bring the powers in question within the operation of some express grant of powers. For illustration I will refer only to two extreme cases—the
Louisiana purchase, and the issue of treasury notes
with the character of legal tender.

In the case of the Louisiana purchase, the exercise
of the questionable power was so plainly beneficial
to the whole country that it was generally acquiesced
in. But the claim of an express or implied power to
make the purchase was so palpably untenable that
the transaction has been tacitly admitted to have
been an actual but necessary violation of the Constitution. Even Mr. Jefferson, to whom the credit of
effecting the purchase of Louisiana was justly and
chiefly due, was of the opinion that there was no
warrant in the Constitution, for the exercise of such
a power, and recommended the adoption of an
amendment to the Constitution ratifying that purchase. In speaking of the objections which were
urged against the project Judge Story says :

" The friends of the measure were driven to the adoption of the
doctrine that the right to acquire territory was incident to national
sovereignty ; that it was a resulting power, growing necessarily out

of the aggregate power confided by the Federal Constitution, that the appropriation might justly be vindicated upon this ground, and also upon the ground that it was for the defence and general welfare." [1]

An equally remarkable case of a strained construction of constitutional provisions is the exercise by Congress of the power to make the United States treasury notes legal tender, in payment of all debts, public and private.

The exercise of this power is not so plainly beneficial; on the contrary, it has been considered by many able publicists to be both an injurious and a wrongful interference with the private rights of the individual. For this reason, the assumption of this power by the National Government has not met with a general acquiescence; and the constitutionality of the acts of Congress, which declared the treasury notes to be legal tender, has been questioned in numerous cases, most of which have found the way to the Supreme Court of the United States. In Hepburn *v.* Griswold,[2] the acts of Congress of 1862 and 1863 were declared to be unconstitutional, so far as they make the treasury notes of the United States legal tender in the payment of pre-existing debts.

---

[1] Story on Constitution, § 1,286. I do not wish it to be inferred that I am unaware of the opinion of Chief-Justice Marshall, that the power to purchase foreign territory is to be implied from the power to make treaties with foreign nations. See Am. Ins. Co. *v.* Canter, 1 Pet., 511, 542. But the claim is made that this is one of the cases in which the doctrine of implied powers has been improperly applied.

[2] 8 Wall., 603.

In the Legal-tender cases,[1] the opinion of the court in Hepburn *v.* Griswold was overruled, and the acts of 1862 and 1863 were declared to be constitutional in making treasury notes legal tender, whether they applied to existing or subsequent debts, the burden of the opinion being that Congress has the right, as a war measure, to give to these notes the character of legal tender. In 1878 Congress passed an act providing for the reissue of the treasury notes, and declared them to be legal tender in payment of all debts. In a case arising under the act of 1878, the Supreme Court of the United States has finally affirmed the opinion announced in 12 Wallace, and held further that the power of the government to make its treasury notes legal tender, whenever the public exigencies require it, being admitted, it becomes a question of legislative discretion when the public welfare requires the exercise of the power.[2] A perusal of these cases will disclose the fact that the members of the court and the attorneys in the causes have not always referred to the same constitutional provisions for the authority to make the treasury notes legal tender. Some have claimed it to be a power implied from the power to levy and carry on war; some refer it to the power to borrow money, while others claim it may be implied from the grant of

---

[1] 12 Wall., 457.   [2] Juillard *v.* Greenman, 110, U. S., 421.

power to coin money and regulate the value of it. It will not be necessary for the present purpose to demonstrate that this power is not a fair implication from the express powers mentioned. A careful reading of all the opinions in the cases referred to will at least throw the matter into hopeless doubt and uncertainty, if it does not convince the reader that in assuming this position violence has been done by the court to the plain literal meaning of the words.

The cases are not rare in which forced construction has been resorted to, in order to justify the exercise of powers which are deemed necessary by public opinion. Nor can we expect to prevent altogether this tendency to strain and force the literal meaning of the written Constitution, in order to bring it into conformity with that unwritten constitution, which is the real constitution, and which embodies the living rules of conduct; for this unwritten constitution is steadily but slowly changing under the pressure of popular opinion and public necessities, checked only by the popular reverence for the written word. But it is wise to eliminate every thing which is calculated to increase this strain; and if the strain is increased in any case by an erroneous interpretation of the grammatical meaning of the written Constitution, it is a public benefit to point this error out, even though it be-

comes necessary to claim that the framers of the
Constitution did not understand the literal meaning
of their own enactment. ' The attempt will be made
to show that this was the case with the accepted interpretation of the Tenth Amendment to the Federal
Constitution.

A stable and enduring government cannot be so
constructed that no branch of it cannot exercise a
given power unless it is granted by the Constitution, expressly or by necessary implication, unless
one escapes from the dilemma by claiming any
valuable power as implied from the power to pro-
mote the general welfare. A government, as a
totality, may properly be compared to a general
agent, who does not require any specific delegation
of power to do an act, provided it falls within the
scope of the agent's general authority. A government, like a general agent, may have express restrictions or limitations upon its general powers. But in
the absence of a prohibition, the right to exercise a
given power, which falls within the legitimate scope
of governmental authority, must be vested in some
branch of the government. As a general proposition, I believe the foregoing statement that all governments can exercise any governmental power,
which is not prohibited, as of necessity, would pass
without question. Criticism is to be expected only
when the attempt is made to apply the doctrine to

the composite federal state. Undertaking the proof of the correctness of this rule, in its application to the federal state, in order to put the whole matter clearly before the reader, I wish, with the aid of a diagram, to classify and distinguish the powers of government in the division of them between the two great parts of the federal state. It is as follows:

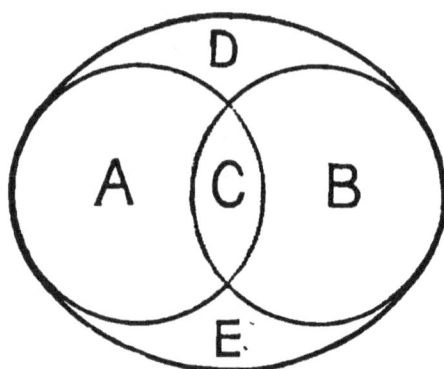

Outer circle represents totality of governmental powers.
Circle A = powers delegated to the United States.
   "   B = powers reserved to the States.
Segment C = concurrent powers.
   "   D = powers prohibited to both branches of government.
   "   E =   "   "   " the States, but neither pro-
hibited nor delegated to the United States.

√ The question for discussion is whether the United States Government may exercise a power which is prohibited to the States, but which is neither prohibited nor delegated to the General Government. The claim is made, on the general principle enunciated above, that from the necessity of the case the

United States Government can exercise such a power, for it would be impossible to construct a government, no branch of which can exercise a necessary power, unless it has been granted. As a proposition of fact, I need only refer to the two cases of governmental action without express authority, heretofore explained, in order to establish its truth. Whatever the written Constitution may provide on this question, the fact is that the United States Government does exercise powers which are not delegated to it by the written Constitution. I do not mean to say that constitutional conventions never attempt to lay down a different rule. On the contrary, if the great men who have contributed to the building up of the American constitutional law have been free from error in their construction of the tenth amendment of the Federal Constitution, the adoption of that amendment was an attempt to do this impossible thing, and the attempt has resulted in repeated violations of the Constitution, as construed by them, by the assumption by Congress of powers which were not expressly delegated nor fairly inplied. The Louisiana purchase and the Legal-tender cases, already referred to, furnish sufficient illustration of the truth of the statement. Cases of the same character will surely arise from time to time, and each repetition will diminish the popular reverence for the written Constitution,—an evil to be deprecated by every earnest jurist. The difficulty in many of the cases lies in the accepted interpretation of the tenth amendment.

According to the prevailing interpretation of that amendment, in order that the United States may by treaty make a purchase of foreign territory, or declare by act of Congress that the treasury notes shall be legal tender in payment of all public and private debts, the power must be granted by the Constitution. It is clear that the State governments cannot exercise these powers, for the exercise of them is expressly prohibited to the States. But if it can be shown that this interpretation of the tenth amendment does not bring out the true grammatical meaning ; that the tenth amendment does not apply to such cases, it must be conceded that the United States may exercise these and other like powers, although they are not expressly or impliedly granted.[1]

There is no reason why the real meaning of that amendment should not be given effect in construing the constitutionality of such acts. For no rule of construction is binding upon the courts and other departments of the government which does not rest for its authority upon some provision of the written Constitution. The intentions of the framers of the

---

[1] It is claimed, however, by the author elsewhere, that the power to make treasury notes legal tender is prohibited by the Constitution to both the United States and the States.—See Tiedeman's " Limitations of Police Power," § 90.

Constitution are not at all binding upon the present generation, except so far as they have been embodied in the written word.[1]

The tenth amendment reads as follows: "The powers, not delegated to the United States by the Constitution, nor prohibited by it to the States, are reserved to the States respectively or to the people." It is clear that, if a given power is not prohibited to the States, the General Government cannot exercise it, unless there is an express delegation of the power. The amendment declares that such powers are reserved to the States or to the people. But if a given power is prohibited to the States, but not delegated to the United States—the right to purchase foreign territory, for example,—can it be said that under this amendment the exercise of this power is reserved to the States? The very prohibition to the States forbids this construction. It may be claimed that in such a case the power would be reserved "to the people." But that claim cannot be sustained. The reservation of the powers (referred to in the amendment) in the alternative "to the States respectively or to the people," evidently involves a consideration of the possibility that the

---

[1] " As men whose intentions require no concealment generally employ the words which most directly and aptly express the idea they intend to convey, the enlightened patriots who framed our Constitution, and the people who adopted it, must be understood to have employed words in their natural sense, and to have intended what they have said."—Marshall, C.-J., in Gibbons *v.* Ogden, 9 Wheat., 1.

State constitutions may prohibit to the States the exercise of a power which is reserved to them under the Federal Constitution, and in that case the power would be reserved to the people. What powers " are reserved to the States respectively, or to the people "? The answer is, those powers which are " *not (neither)* delegated to the United States by the Constitution, *nor* prohibited by it to the States." These two clauses, which contain the exceptions to the operation of the amendment, are not in the alternative. In order that it may be claimed under this amendment that a power is " reserved to the States respectively or to the people," it must avoid both exceptions, *i.e.*, it must be a power, which is *neither* delegated to the United States *nor* prohibited to the States. It cannot be successfully claimed that a power is reserved, which is prohibited to the States, but which is not delegated to the United States. The conclusion, therefore, is that the United States Government is one of enumerated powers, so far that it cannot exercise any power which is not prohibited by the Constitution to the States, unless it is expressly or impliedly delegated to the United States. But those powers, which are prohibited to the States, and which fall legitimately within the scope of governmental authority, may be exercised by the United States, unless they are also prohibited to the United States.

There need not be any express or implied grant of such powers to the United States.

It is not claimed or implied that the interpretation of the tenth amendment here advocated conforms more nearly to the intentions of the framers of the Constitution than that which has been generally accepted by writers upon the constitutional law of the country. Indeed, the revelation of the presence in the early history of the United States, of forces of disintegration in the politics of the country, equal or almost equal to the forces of consolidation, would incline one to suppose that the intentions of the law-makers in the formation of the Constitution were properly reflected in that construction of constitutional limitations which would most effectively hamper and curtail the powers of the national government. The great struggle of the wise men of those days was to secure for the Federal Government the delegation of sufficient power to establish an independent government; and it may be said with equal truth and force that the Federal Constitution was wrested from an unwilling people. It would therefore be impossible to show that this construction of the tenth amendment was in conformity with the intentions and expectations of those whose votes enacted it. It is freely admitted that the prevailing interpretation is without doubt what the framers of the amendment intended.

But the intentions of our ancestors cannot be permitted to control the present activity of the government, where they have not been embodied in the habits of thought of the people—we have seen that the interpretation has been practically ignored in the two illustrative cases—or in the written word of the Constitution. Where the written word is equally susceptible of two constructions, one of which reflects more accurately the intentions of the power that speaks through the word, that construction must prevail. Now the living power, whose will is given expression in the written word, is not the men who framed or voted for the written word, but the present possessors of political power. The present popular will must indicate which shade of meaning must be given to the written word. And that interpretation becomes the only possible one, when it may be shown by the experience of a century, that the alternative construction, which reflects the intentions of the original enactors of the written word, is pernicious to the stability of the government, and in violation of the soundest principles of political science.

CHAPTER XI.

CARDINAL RULE OF INTERPRETATION AND CON-STRUCTION OF WRITTEN CONSTITUTIONS.

IT is a noteworthy fact, that in the earlier stages of development of a system of jurisprudence, when the knowledge of the meaning of words is crudest and least certain, greater stress is laid in interpretation upon the letter of the law than in the more advanced judicial age. The written word is held in reverential awe, and is treated as containing every element of the law.[1] This tendency, in the inquiry into the operation and meaning of writings, to confine one's attention to the written word, is without doubt caused by a popular ignorance of the real

---

[1] " A close adherence to the letter is a mark of unripeness everywhere, and especially so in law. The history of law might write over its first chapter, as a motto, ' In the beginning was the word.' To all rude peoples the word appears something mysterious, whether it be written or solemnly uttered as a formula, and their simple faith fills it with supernatural power." v. Ihering, " Geist des R. Rechts," Bd. II., Theil 2, p. 441. In the subsequent pages Prof. v. Ihering undertakes an elaborate explanation of the metaphysical origin of the two kinds of interpretation, which is not only attractive for its beauty, but also for its value to the jurist.

character of words as " vehicles of thought." The
object of all communications is to enable one mind
to learn the thoughts of the other; and the popular
notion is that the spoken or written word is literally
the " vehicle of thought "; that the thought is actually conveyed by the word from one mind to another. Of course this is altogether false. Thought
is a mental operation, and the intended effect of
words is to reproduce the same operation in the
brain of another. But the word does not impart or
transmit the movement from one brain to the
other. It is also true that words are not the
only means of communication of thought. Smiles,
frowns, nods of the head, winks, and all kinds of
gesturing, serve to communicate thought often as
well as words; and where the words are accom-
panied by such gestures, their meaning is often
materially modified, and sometimes completely
changed. To take note under such circumstances
simply of the spoken word would give to the mind
of the hearer a very wrong impression of the thought
of the speaker, and hence the actual thought would
not have been communicated. In other words, the
movements in the brain of the writer or speaker
would not be accurately reproduced in the brain
of the reader or hearer. Words, therefore, when
considered separate from surrounding circumstances,
do not always act as reliable vehicles of thought.

To secure at all times a correct appreciation of
the meaning of the writer or speaker, one must
take into consideration every fact, external and
internal, which exerted an influence upon him at the
time of writing or speaking—his characteristics as
well as his environment,—for a word used by one
man does not necessarily have the same shade of
meaning which it might have when used by another.
But every word must be understood roughly to have
a certain and common meaning; else it would be
impossible for one mind to communicate with
another. But within the limits of the general meaning of a word, there may be, and usually are, various
shades of meaning, which the word alone cannot un-
fold, and which must be learned from other sources.
Now the literal or grammatical interpretation can
only disclose this rough general meaning; while the
finer shades of meaning are only brought out by a
liberal or logical interpretation, *i.e.*, by a consideration of every fact, having more or less connection
with, and influence over, the writer. It is needless
to add that the latter interpretation is alone relied
upon by educated peoples.

Applying these fundamental principles to the
interpretation of constitutional and statutory law, it
may be stated that in the pursuit of the meaning of
the law, every fact or circumstance, surrounding the
lawgiver, when the law was promulgated, is required

by our rules of interpretation to be inquired into; so that the cardinal rule of interpretation of laws may be said to be, that the intention of the law-giver, when the law was enacted, must prevail. The same rule of interpretation is made to apply to statutes and constitutions, as is applied to private contracts.

In recognition of the soundness of this rule, as explained by our books upon constitutional and statutory construction, we expect a law to be enforced in the sense in which the legislators intended, whether the legislators be members of a constitutional convention or of an ordinary legislature; and the student is directed, in his effort to ascertain the meaning of a statute or clause of a constitution, to read the history of the times, the journal of the convention or legislature, and the speeches of its members. From these extraneous sources one expects to learn every thing necessary to an understanding of the exact meaning of the lawgiver.

But would a strict observance of this rule enable a student to get an accurate knowledge of what the law is now? If the illustrations heretofore given in support of my thesis teach any one thing with precision, it is that the intention of the legislator, whether he be Congressman or a member of a constitutional convention, is only effectuated, so far as it has found lodgment in the written word. The written word stands alone as the embodiment of his intention; and if it is possible for the court, in the enforcement of the law, to find in the written word two or more shades of meaning, it does not enforce that shade of meaning which was intended by the lawgiver, but that shade which best reflects the prevalent sense of right. And, in securing that concordance of the written law and the prevalent sense of right, all these rules of interpretation as generally understood are thrown to the winds.[1] Even the ordinary and plain meanings are twisted out of the words; and, although public opinion usually commands an adherence to the word, if the case should be distressing, and the necessity for a repudiation of the written word be great, in obedience to popular demands, it is done by governmental authority. Still, as explained in the first chapter, the cases are rare in which a court safely disregards the written word of the legislature, for the prevalent sense of

---

[1] " No statute ever resisted, in the end, the unfavorable opinion of the profession. Whether he intends it or not, the judge's hand grows weak, the arm of justice loses its power, acute interpretation lends all its means to evade and undermine such a statute, to introduce conditions not found in the text or to contract its language, and, as it were, by a silent conspiracy, to invent and recommend the most forced constructions, till even the rules of logic bend to the claims of interest. This silent war of the profession against the positive law is repeated wherever that law becomes out of date without being formally repealed. It is in this manner that our instincts of right naturally react against the legislator's disregard of them."—Lieber's " Hermeneutics," Appendix, by Dr. Hammond, pp. 272, 273.

right usually requires a strict observance of the written word, however much violence is done by interpretation to the plain intention of the legislator.

Is it a sufficient explanation of the common disregard of legislative intention to say that it is due to the influence of the imperfections of human nature on the administration of the law? To my mind the fault lies in the cardinal rule of interpretation, as given by all our writers. It is true that a true interpretation of the law must disclose the real and full meaning of the lawgiver; but in countries in which popular governments are established the real lawgiver is not the man or body of men which first enacted the law ages ago; it is the people of the present day who possess the political power, and whose commands give life to what otherwise is a dead letter. No people are ruled by dead men, or by the utterances of dead men. Those utterances are only law so far as they are voiced by some living power. Hence, since under a popular government governmental authority rests upon the voice of the people, or the voice of that part of the people which moulds public opinion, that interpretation, in strict conformity with the fundamental rule of interpretation, must prevail which best reflects the prevalent sense of right. For the present possessors of political power, and not their predecessors, are the lawgivers for the present generation. While, therefore, as a

general rule, the written word remains unchanged
and confines the operations of the popular will to a
choice of the shades of meaning, of which the written
word is capable—until the written word has been
repealed or modified by the proper authority,—the
practical operation of the law will vary with each
change in the prevalent sense of right; and the judge
or practitioner of the law, who would interpret the
law rightly, *i.e.*, ascertain with precision the rule of
conduct in any case, need not concern himself so
much with the intentions of the framers of the Constitution or statute, as with the modifications of the
written word by the influence of the present will of
the people. Or, in other words, he must find out
what the possessors of political power now mean by
the written word.

This is not a philosophical speculation, having no
foundation in fact. Notwithstanding its apparently
radical contradiction of the commonly accepted rules
of interpretation, it is acted upon and recognized by
all the leading American authorities. Dr. Lieber recognizes this factor—unconsciously, it is true,—when,
in distinguishing between the interpretation and construction of constitutional provisions, he says that a
constitutional " sentence, then, must be *interpreted*,
if we are desirous to ascertain what precise meaning
the framers of our Constitution attached to it, and
construed, if we are desirous of knowing how they

would have understood it respecting new relations, which they could not have known at the time, and which, nevertheless, fall decidedly within the province of this provision."[1]   And the same may be said of Chief-Justice Marshall, where, in his opinion in the Dartmouth College case, he claims that a case may come within the operation of a constitutional provision, even though the framers of the Constitution did not anticipate it, provided there is nothing in the written word to indicate that they would have excluded it if it had been anticipated.[2]

If a law or constitutional provision can by construction be made to cover a case, which the enacter

[1] "Hermeneutics," p. 168.

[2] "It is more than possible that the preservation of rights of this description was not particularly in the view of the framers of the Constitution, when the clause under consideration (the provision against impairment of obligation of contracts) was introduced into that instrument. It is probable that interferences of more frequent occurrence, to which the temptation was stronger, and of which the mischief was more extensive, constituted the great motive for imposing this restriction on the State legislatures. But although a particular and rare case may not, in itself, be of sufficient magnitude to induce a rule, yet it may be governed by the rule when established, unless some plain and strong reason for excluding it can be given. It is not enough to say that this particular case was not in the mind of the convention when the article was framed, nor of the American people when it was adopted. It is necessary to go further and to say that had this particular case been suggested the language would have been so varied as to exclude it, or it would have been made a special exception. The case being within the words of the rule, must be within its operations likewise, unless there be something in its literal construction so obviously absurd or mischievous, or repugnant to the general spirit of the instrument, as to justify those who expounded the Constitution in making it an exception."—4 Wheat., pp. 644, 645.

of the law or provision did not and could not anticipate, and which he consequently cannot be said to
have intended to include within the operation of the
rule, then by what will power is the law or constitutional provision made to apply to that case? Is it
not the present will of the people? And is not,
then, in accordance with the rules laid down by
Marshall and Lieber, a law or constitutional rule
made to mean what the popular will intends by the
written word? The real character of the rule cannot
be changed by giving it the name of construction.
Construction, as defined by the authorities and distinguished from interpretation, is nothing more than
that logical interpretation, whereby the real meaning
of the living lawgiver, *i.e.*, the present possessors of
political power, is ascertained.

This fallacy in interpretation of laws is the result
of holding on to a rule, after a change of circumstances has confused its meaning or made its application misleading; and its retention, after it has
ceased to be true, is due to the general acceptation
of the groundless doctrine of the social contract.
Under this doctrine, as well as under the doctrine of
the divine right of kings, the popular conception of
law was, as indicated in Blackstone's definition, that
it emanated from some power above and beyond us,
from God in the one case, and from our ancestors in
the other case. That being the source of the law, in

order to ascertain what the law is, we must discover what the governmental representatives of God, or of our ancestors, meant by the words used in their enactments; in the same manner as we endeavor to ascertain the intentions of parties to a private contract, in order to determine their contractual rights. But as soon as we recognize the present will of the people as the living source of law, we are obliged, in construing the law, to follow, and give effect to, the present intentions and meaning of the people.

CHAPTER XII.

THE REAL VALUE OF WRITTEN CONSTITUTIONS.

IF it be true, as the foregoing pages indicate, that all political constitutions undergo a constant and gradual evolution, keeping pace with the development of civilization, whether there be a written constitution or not ; that these changes generally take place without formal amendments to the written constitution, the question would naturally arise: Of what value then is a written constitution which demonstrates its superiority over an unwritten constitution? The student who has been in the habit —which is still very common, if not universal, with practical lawyers and judges—of beginning his inquiry into constitutional law with the fundamental postulate that all constitutional rules have their root in the written declarations of the sovereign power, and that these declarations must be observed and obeyed in the spirit and meaning with which they were first promulgated,—such a student is apt, if he concedes the truth of the present thesis, to conclude that the superiority of written over purely unwritten constitutions has been dissipated altogether.

Not so. There is still room for the claim that the written constitution has in it elements which fundamentally change the character of the government, and which the unwritten constitution cannot possibly claim. Not only this, but the further claim may be substantiated that, with a full understanding of the real value of written constitutions, and a differentiation of that real value from its supposed but fictitious value, the superiority of written over purely unwritten constitutions is enhanced rather than diminished.

In the pursuit of this inquiry, it is necessary, as elsewhere, to take cognizance of the existence and effect of the two opposing social forces, which are present everywhere in bodies-politic, and which were prominently distinguishable at the time when the present Federal Constitution was adopted, viz.: the force of consolidation or centralization, and the force of disintegration. In every body-politic, in the effort to reconcile the claims of legal order and personal freedom from restraint, there are those who, on the one hand, are willing to sacrifice personal liberty to the cause of law and order, only as far as this sacrifice is absolutely necessary to the public safety; while, on the other hand, there are those who place so high a value upon law and order, that they are willing and are clamorous for the sacrifice of personal liberty, whenever that sacrifice promotes the public welfare. The first class of political units translate the Latin maxim, *salus populi suprema lex*, the *safety* of the people is the highest law; while the second class understand by that maxim that the *welfare* of the people is the highest law. The first class are therefore always afraid of the tyranny of officials; while the second class dread the power of the *demos.* The first class are anxious to impose restraints upon the power of the officials; while the second class are anxious to diminish as far as possible the influence of the people on legislation. The first class are thoroughly democratic in spirit; the second class, thoroughly aristocratic.

It is needless to state that both of these political classes were present in full force during the first years of our national existence. In the sense in which the terms have here been explained, George Washington, Alexander Hamilton, James Madison, John Randolph, and others, who took the same view of politics, were Aristocrats; while Samuel Adams, George Clinton, Thomas Jefferson, Patrick Henry, etc., were Democrats. The Aristocrats, dreading the absolutism of a democratic majority, sought to establish a government, which, although representative and popular in character, could be conducted and controlled by the better elements of society, and whose actual administration would be as free as possible from the influence of the masses. Hence, in the constitutional convention, they proposed the establishment of a strong national government, with such checks and safeguards thrown around the exercise of the power of amendment, as to give permanency to the form and character of the government, and to prevent radical changes in response to every popular clamor. The Democrats were, on the other hand, in constant fear of the establishment in this country of another George III., under the guise of a popular executive. They fought for their liberties step by step, the result of the contest being that the Federal Constitution became a collection of compromises. But, in order that the opposing element may not easily or inadvertently secure any increase of power for the Federal Government, the Democrats were likewise anxious to impose restraints upon the power of amendment. Both parties then concurred in the same conclusion, proceeding from opposite standpoints, and resting the conclusions upon different reasons.

But in their desire to impose restraints upon the exercise of official and popular power, respectively, they did not stop with making it difficult to amend the Constitution. Legislation was also made difficult by dividing the legislative power between three different independent bodies or departments of the government, the President, the Senate, and the House of Representatives, and requiring the concurrence of all, in order to make new laws, or to change existing ones,—except that the two houses of Congress were permitted, by a two-thirds vote in each house, to pass a law over the veto of the President.

The further provision is made, in the procurement of the same ends, that the President, the members of the Senate, and of the House of Representatives, shall not all be elected at the same time. Taken as a whole, it was the most ingenious device for the prevention of legislation that the world has ever known; and after the adoption of the Constitution, both parties, from their respective standpoints, extolled these features of the Constitution, perhaps beyond their true value, losing sight of the great loss which en-sues from unwise legislation, because of the supreme difficulty to secure its repeal or modification.[1]

But all these checks and balances, set down in a written constitution, would be unavailing, if the

---

[1] John Adams has enumerated these checks and balances as follows: "First, the States are balanced against the general government. Second, the House of Representatives is balanced against the Senate, and the Senate against the House. Third, the executive authority is in some degree balanced against the legislature. Fourth, the judiciary is balanced against the legislature, the executive, and the State governments. Fifth, the Senate is balanced against the President in all appointments to office, and in all treaties. Sixth, the people hold in their own hands the balance against their own representatives by periodical elections. Seventh, the legislatures of the several States are balanced against the Senate by sexennial elections. Eighth, the electors are balanced against the people in their choice of President and Vice-President."—Letter of John Adams to John Taylor, "Works," vi., 467.

means of securing their observance were not likewise provided in the exalted and extraordinary power of the courts to declare when a law, passed by Congress, or an act, committed by an official, is in contradiction of some provision of the Constitution. There is no express grant to the courts of such a power; it is simply deduced from the necessity of determining when there is a conflict which law they must apply to the cause of action, the law of Congress or the rule of the Constitution. Hence the courts have no authority to pass upon the constitutionality of legislation, except when the settlement of this question is necessary in deciding the issue of a *bona-fide* cause of action, brought before the court by *bona-fide* litigants. But whenever it becomes in this way necessary to pass upon the constitutionality of national and State legislation, the decision of the court is binding upon all the parties to the suit, and upon all others whose rights are in any way affected by the judgment of the court.

The same dread of the possession of absolute power by any department of the government is to be observed in the limitations of this extraordinary judicial power. The Supreme Court of the United States is not placed by the Constitution above the other departments of the government, with the power to prohibit any unconstitutional exercise of power by them. Not at all. This power to pass upon the constitutionality of a law or official act is only acquired by the court as an incident of its duty . to enforce the law between parties litigant. The judgment of the United States Supreme Court on a constitutional question is not binding upon the President or upon Congress. Each department is required to obey the Constitution, according to the light in which the question under discussion is viewed by it. Andrew Jackson vetoed the bill providing for the maintenance of a system of banks by the Federal Government, on the ground that the bill was unconstitutional, although the Supreme Court had pronounced a similar bill to be within the constitutional power of Congress. Furthermore, Mr. Jefferson refused to obey the order of the court in Marbury *v.* Madison (1 Cranch, 137 [1]), while Mr. Lincoln ignored the opinion of Chief-Justice Taney,[2] that the presidential proclamation of the suspension of the writ of *habeas corpus* was an unconstitutional exercise of authority. This is not all. The Supreme Court is still further shorn of its power by giving

---

[1] In this case, Mr. Madison, as Secretary of State under President Jefferson, had refused to issue the commission of one Marbury, who had been appointed to a judicial position by President Adams on the last day of his term of office, but who had not received his commission of the retiring President. The Supreme Court undertook to compel the new Secretary of State to issue the commission, but the mandamus was ignored by the President and his Secretary.

[2] In *Ex parte* Merryman, Taney's Circuit Decisions, Campbell's Rep., 246.

to Congress the power to increase the number of the Supreme Court judges, and thus, with the aid of the President, to change the composition and tendencies of the court. If at any time the Supreme Court should too persistently withstand any popular demand in a case in which the people will not submit to the judicial negative, by an increase in the number of the judges and the appointment to the newly created judgeships of men who will do the people's bidding, the popular will may be realized.

I do not think there can be much doubt that the danger of official tyranny has been successfully dissipated in the American constitutional system,—except so far as such tyranny may be demanded by a popular majority,—by the frequency of the elections and the short terms of service. Officials of all classes are too anxious to secure popular approval to make the administration of their offices a popular menace. They have their fingers constantly upon the public pulse, and every expression of popular approval and disapproval is noted. Indeed, the direct and constant responsibility of almost all classes of officials to public opinion, through frequent popular elections, goes very far towards nullifying any superior merit which the written constitution possesses over an unwritten constitution. For these officials, instead of attempting to throttle the popular will, are too ready to obey every popular caprice, it matters not how grievously the written Constitution may be thereby violated. And were the judges of the federal bench elected for short terms of service, and by popular election, as is the case in many of the States with respect to the State judiciary, the written Constitution would serve very little purpose. It is not needed for the protection of the people against the tyranny of the officials; its only value is to serve as a check upon the popular will in the interest of the minority. By making the federal judiciary hold office during good behavior, and by providing in the Constitution for one Supreme Court, which cannot be abolished by congressional action, the means have been provided, in ordinary times of peace, of protecting the minority against the absolutism of a democratic majority. It enables a small body of distinguished men, whose life-long career is calculated to produce in them an exalted love of justice and an intelligent appreciation of the conflicting rights of individuals, and the life-tenure of whose offices serves to withdraw them from all fear of popular disapproval; it enables these independent, right-minded men, in accordance with the highest law, to plant themselves upon the provisions of the written Constitution, and deny to popular legislation the binding force of law, whenever such legislation infringes a constitutional provision. This is the real value of the written Constitution. It

legalizes, and therefore makes possible and successful, the opposition to the popular will.

But this opposition, when most successful, does
not serve as a complete barrier to the popular will.
Not only do the judges themselves fall under the
influence of the prevalent sense of right, and ordi-
narily give in their decisions an accurate expression
of it, but the various checks upon this veto power
of the courts also serve to make their action only
a dilatory proceeding ; or, to adopt the happy
expression of James Russell Lowell,[1] this over-
ruling power of the Supreme Court of the United
States is but an obstacle " in the way of the
people's whim, not of their will." But with this
limitation, extensive as it is, the written Constitution
serves a most beneficent purpose. If one professes
any faith at all in popular government, he must
confess to a desire that the popular will shall prevail,
and that the danger to the commonwealth lies not
in the people's will but in their whims and ill-con-
sidered wishes. And even if the student does not
have any faith in popular government, he must
admit that, with an enlightened and spirited people, who know their strength, and who know that
the living power in all municipal law proceeds from
them, it is an absolute impossibility to suppress the
popular will. Happy is that country whose consti-

---

[1] "Democracy, and Other Addresses" (1887), p. 24.

tutional system enables it to enjoy the blessings of popular government, while at the same time it is protected from the evils of hasty and passionate legislation. And while, perhaps, the constitutional system of this country has not developed exactly in accordance with the wishes and expectations of Washington, Hamilton, Madison, and their co-workers, yet if it were possible for them to know the results actually achieved, they would be satisfied with the knowledge that they had in a measure succeeded in establishing, what exists nowhere else, a popular government without democratic absolutism.

THE END.

www.ingramcontent.com/pod-product-compliance
Lightning Source LLC
Chambersburg PA
CBHW020544270326
41927CB00006B/715